EDUCATIONAL COMPUTING

EDUCATIONAL COMPUTING

Issues, Trends and a Practical Guide

By

DENNIS M. ADAMS

MARY FUCHS

CHARLES C THOMAS • PUBLISHER

Springfield • Illinois • U.S.A.

Published and Distributed Throughout the World by

CHARLES C THOMAS • PUBLISHER
2600 South First Street
Springfield, Illinois 62717

ISBN 0-398-05213-1

Library of Congress Catalog Card Number: 85-28891

With THOMAS BOOKS *careful attention is given to all details of manufacturing and design. It is the Publisher's desire to present books that are satisfactory as to their physical qualities and artistic possibilities and appropriate for their particular use.* THOMAS BOOKS *will be true to those laws of quality that assure a good name and good will.*

Printed in the United States of America
Q-R-3

Library of Congress Cataloging in Publication Data

Adams, Dennis M.
Educational computing.

Bibliography: p.
1. Education—Data processing. 2. Computer-assisted instruction. 3. Education—Data processing—Teacher training. 4. Computer-assisted instruction—Teacher training. I. Fuchs, Mary. II. Title.
LB1028.43.A34 1986 370'.28'5 85-28891
ISBN 0-398-05213-1

INTRODUCTION

SCHOOLS ARE FACED with training old **and** new teachers in the use of the new technologies. In our survey of the field we found that teacher training institutions are just beginning to require their perspective teachers to have training in computer use. Presently, course offerings in this area are made up primarily of classes in **"Educational Computing," "Computers in the Classroom,"** and **"New Computer-Based Instructional Technologies."** Teachers need assistance in all of these, but just as importantly need courses that deal with technology assessment, future studies, and the societal implications of the new technology.

Without their asking for it, a major responsibility for teaching teachers about computing has fallen into the lap of the school districts themselves. This book is intended as a guide for both **preservice** and **inservice** teachers—providing a working knowledge of the fast moving educational computing field. With both preservice and inservice needs in mind, we have tried to strike a balance between an educational computing reference manual and a discussion of the issues and trends in the field. The intention is to provide a practical guide to computing issues for those interested in the education process—whether inservice teachers, college students in the teacher preparation process, administrators, or parents who need help in bringing educational software into the home.

Some teachers may not know a disk drive from the central processing unit. However, many educators today have gone well past the point where they need the definition of **monitor**, or instructions about how to put software into the computer's disk drive. There are ideas, information and suggestions here for both groups. Whether they are aware of the basics of computing or not, educators want ideas of how to better integrate computers into their curriculum. And they want to take part in the discussions about where the technology is leading. Teachers have no alternative but to accept the responsibility of being key decision-makers—determining the role of the educational microcomputer in this swiftly moving, and sometimes confusing, field. It is after all, the teacher who is most aware of that key variable: **the characteristics of effective instruction**. No matter how advanced the technology becomes it will always come back to our discipline—curriculum and instruction.

Educational Computing: Issues, Trends and a Practical Guide is an idea book relating practice, theory, and research to new technological possibilities. The intention is to give teachers at many skill levels a knowledge of the conceptional issues, as well as actual possibilities for instructional practice. Therefore issues are interspersed with practical ideas. Concepts are presented so that individuals new to computing can begin, and those who are very knowledgeable about educational computing can find something new.

In discussing complex educational and technical matters there is always a tension between the "novice" and the "expert"—between "clarity" and "truth." Although research and theory are important considerations and are taken seriously, the book is not constructed like an article in a scholarly research journal. Rather, the intention is to interpret research findings along with practical applications for a broader audience—presenting different and controversial points of view for discussion purposes. Every effort is made to provide a means for getting everybody past the "benign neglect" that best describes the technological establishment's attitude towards the public's understanding of technology.

Both the experienced computer educator and someone who has never touched a computer will find this a useful text—both in and outside of the classroom. Getting the hardware is only the beginning. Everything from what to look for in educational software to specific "off line" activities not requiring the presence of a computer are provided. Computers are approached as "tools to think with." The intent is to help those interested in instruction learn about educational computing, computer-based telecommunications, artificial intelligence, and computer-related social issues. All of the material in this book is designed to help educators tap computer controlled technologies in ways that will positively influence what is occurring in the classroom. The same principles will apply to parents who want to make educational use of computers in the home. The tone of the book reflects the fact that computer-based technology is becoming easier for teachers, students, and parents to use.

We have arranged for key concepts to be set up for both independent and group work—with practical lessons for different skill and age levels.

Introduction Ideas are arranged in a manner that allows a teacher operating independently, a peer workshop leader, or a college level instructor to structure the computer related learning experiences. There are sections on software evaluation, hardware, practical student activities, social implications, mergers with other technologies, telecommunications, programming, and artificial intelligence.

Educators at every level need to be aware that computers can help solve some difficult teaching problems that other methods cannot solve. Drawing on personal experiences of educational computing workshop leaders, the emphasis of this book is on process and **meaning**. "Computer literacy" is not viewed as a substitute for the technological understanding that all of our citizens need. Therefore societal issues are incorporated and discussed along with the computing technology curriculum. Ideas for using both computing hardware and software are provided. And the future direction that computer technology may take is evaluated so that teachers can explore the technological horizons in education and prepare their students for an ever changing world.

A teaching tool as powerful as the microcomputer cannot be neutral. It will alter both how we feel about learning and how we teach. Our developing technological marvels could let children experience things they might not be able to understand through other media. Computer-based technology can help students visit places (relevant to their studies) that are placed out of reach by time, distance, or danger.

We recognize the fact that once microcomputer technology is introduced into a school there must be adequate support for teachers. Teachers need support in assisting children as they create microworlds and use the computer to explore other powerful instructional ideas. This book sets out to assist in that process—relating interactive educational computing to the reader's own experiences and providing an understanding of how learning can benefit from building an awareness of—and using—computer-based technology.

CONTENTS

EDUCATIONAL COMPUTING

CHAPTER 1

COMPUTER-BASED TECHNOLOGY: ON THE EDGE OF SOMETHING VERY IMPORTANT

TECHNOLOGY OF one type or another has been around for thousands of years. It can now make life better, worse or destroy it altogether. It is the positive human potentials that schools can, and should, exploit. The issues involved in educational computing are not just technological or scientific in nature. They involve philosophy, education, psychology, politics, ethics, the arts, and the humanities. On a practical level, value-free science alone may be valueless for children asking about right and wrong. Yet all sorts of ethical and moral issues confront our use of science and technology. We are living through a real transformation simlar to changes that occurred during the Industrial Revolution: there were shifts in all areas before nearly anyone realized it. It was impossible to stop and before most people knew what was happening machines had transformed the Western world. Once such a major shift occurs there is no going back to the way it was.

These radical shifts didn't negate the previous changes (after all we are still building on the pre-historic Agricultural Revolution). And new technological forces do **not** necessarily build on the concept of older ones in a linear march towards controlling reality. Institutional forces—whether it's funding the Manhatten Project, the Apollo Program, the space shuttle, or the "Star Wars" scheme—have as much to do with shaping new fields of technological and scientific inquiry as do reason, observation, scientific method, or "the search for truth."

Computer-based technology is fundamentally different from previous technology. The permanent changes that computers bring are as important as the Agricultural and Industrial Revolutions of the past. Computers are also the key technology for the future biotechnology "revolution."

Figure 1.

"Would you please tell me which way I ought to go from here?"
"That depends a good deal on where you want to get to," said the Cat.
"I don't much care where—," said Alice.
"Then it doesn't matter which way you go," said the Cat.
"So long as I get somewhere," Alice added as an explanation.
"Oh, you're sure to do that," said the Cat, "if you only walk long enough."

Digitized photograph from **Alice in Wonderland**.

Computing confronts educators today with unique problems and opportunities as they prepare both themselves and their students for participation in a technologically intensive future. As teachers set out on the path of computer awareness, a good first step is to explore how computers are changing our social institutions (including education) and our world. We must not only survive and react to change, but be able to take control—making informed choices, creative applications, and bringing an educator's sensibilities to the machines. A good beginning would be to look at how computers can influence the world, the community, and how they can help us open a window of opportunity for improving our schools.

REVITALIZING EDUCATION IN THE ELECTRONIC AGE

We are well into the electronic age and computers are changing for better or worse, how we do things in the classroom. Unfortunately, never have so many known so little about so much. This is not only true of teachers—other people and our society are both tantalized and terrified by interaction with computers. When you bring a computer into the classroom, things naturally change. Some changes can be anticipated; others cannot. Some changes are desirable; others are not. Of one thing we can be certain, whatever our field of work, we must be aware of the influence of technology or be beached by this sea of change.

New levels of human-computer communication can even help reinvigorate the branches of the mythical tree of knowledge. This has implications that reach beyond the technology and into every sector of society. Psychological comfort, aesthetic pleasure, economic renewal and opportunities for learning are all part of the mix.

Computer technology is finding its way into every aspect of our lives—and schools are not an exception. And although there have been a few connections (primarily at the secondary school level) between computers and schools over the last twenty years, it is only in the last five years that we have seen an explosion of educational computing. Hopefully, the computers' presence in education settings will cause us to think not just more about computers but also more about education.

Either by intention or default educators are involved in curriculum reform. It may be best to begin by considering what should be taught by computers and what should not; why computers increase student motivation to learn; how computer-related activities can be integrated into the curriculum; how to go beyond simplistic drill and practice; how to accommodate the exponential growth of new knowledge; and, generally, how to prepare for a new "learning society" made possible by the computer presence. Simulation, video conferencing, laboratory experimentation, problem solving, writing/reading, and creative/artistic projects via the computer already are available to help frame the answers to these questions.

Few curriculum innovations have moved into schools as quickly as educational computing. Before anyone had time for planning, microcomputers were in place and functioning. Schools are in no position to stop the technological explosion—but they do have the chances to control the direction of the blast. This can be done by drawing on the self-energizing character of this innovative technology, by integrating this new tool into present curriculum, or both.

COMPUTERS ARE COMING FROM THE BASIC ROOTS UP—RATHER THAN FROM THE GENERAL STAFF DOWN

Teachers do not have to be drafted into educational computing. Microcomputer technology is an innovation that students, teachers, and parents are bringing into the schools. This is very different than the usual approach of the state or school district requiring something from above. This difference is important, because it is through teachers experimenting with microcomputers that new methods and curriculum will evolve. This is one of the reasons why we suggest that teachers be taken seriously in the planning process—and why we suggest that teachers be allowed to take computers home with them when school is not in session.

More and more educators are connecting with this powerful learners tool and coming to see the computer as a device they can control. A technological awareness is developing that reflects the interests of students and educators alike. Teachers are even capitalizing on students' expertise and enlisting parents in the effort. Schools are already tapping the instructional benefits of educational computing—in diverse ways. And since no one is sure what computer education **should** be, these different approaches and experiments may be the best way to explore what educational computing **can** be.

ARTIFICIAL INTELLIGENCE (AI)

In addition to teaching basic curriculum skills, there are new (artificially intelligent) programs that allow computers to make a big contribution to defining and thinking about various problems. We are just getting the first microcomputer programs that can reason. Everything from updating our schools to reinvigorating our basic industries will require a reliance on large-scale integration of machine intelligence and knowledge technology. By incorporating the two, the next generation of computers will give their developers an enormous technological, geopolitical and commercial advantage. As a nation we are just starting to realize that whomever controls the information revolution has some form of increased control.

Small start-up companies like Tecnowledge, Intellicorp, and the Carnegie Group are beginning to bring new AI expert systems to the marketplace. Larger companies like Hewlett-Packard, IBM, G.E., and Digital Equipment are also developing products, known as expert systems, that collect, organize and make decision suggestions. Hewlett-Packard is already using such AI systems (that have implications for schools) to more efficiently train workers in their semi conductor manufacturing division.

Just as the Industrial Revolution levered man's muscle power, the computer revolution is in the process of levering our mental powers. We are now capable of building computers that are very nearly self-replicating and can themselves be used to build even smarter and more powerful machines. Intelligence, as we know it, has slowly evolved using DNA as its base. Some of the Magi of computing see a new intelligence emerging—one that does not require a specialized environment providing air, water, and nutrients. Computers do not have to go to school, they learn by simply linking and sharing information and knowledge at the speed of light. Just as airplanes do not fly on the same principles as birds, artificial thinking may progress into something very different from our own biologically based intelligence. As you might guess, the leading edge of computer science has no fixed laws and is highly experimental. In fact, it is akin to a black art. As an "art" it is radically altering our conception of what scientific progress is—and our ideas about how science and technology evolve. Computers do indeed have the power to redefine the relationship of humans to nature and reality.

Artificial Intelligence (AI) is the field that aims to understand how computers can be made to exhibit intelligence. Robotics is part of AI—

and to be "intelligent" robots need to reason, plan, and take action on those plans. And it is **action** that is the key word here.

ROBOTICS

Robots are the most popular symbols of the new computer controlled technologies that are moving quickly throughout the economy. Robotics is the intelligent connection of AI perception to action, forcing artificial intelligence to deal with real objects in the real world. Few technologies have had more impact on people's imaginations than the computerized robot. Even the U.S. Census Bureau has decided to count robots along with humans in their population count. (It turns out that the largest percentage of them work in the auto industry as welders, painters and assemblers). Simplified extensions of this new computer controlled technology are also making inroads into our classrooms. Classroom robots can generally be programmed by students to perform certain tasks. Much of this is simply an illusion of true robotics. But since the "robots" move in direct response to student programs, they make programming and debugging procedures very concrete and immediate.

Educational policy makers should be more concerned about the societal spin-offs from robotized high technology—and technological awareness—than about preparing students in the handful of new high-tech jobs. We are already in the process of having real robots take the place of humans on assembly lines and in certain kinds of dangerous inner and outer space work.

Humans with a broad knowledge base have proven to have the best insurance against obsolescence. Today's workers need to be able to function in an information-intensive, word-oriented, work environment. A well rounded education, the capacity to change and a willingness to learn new concepts is the best foundation in these times of rapid economic changes. Robots have taken over welding and painting jobs at GM and Ford. The best human welder takes the robot through the paces the first time—the welder's skills become obsolete as soon as the robot understands. The computer-controlled robot goes on day and night for years (without the need for coffee breaks, proper ventilation, or even light). Expert welders say that if they (the robots) get it right the first time, they will weld right every time.

Robots have explored the ocean bottom and outer space. The Soviet Union, for example, has demonstrated models of robot spacecraft

Figure 2. Computer Composite Image.

designed to land on Phobas (one of two smaller Martian moons) and hop around like a mechanical frog—using lasers and other sensors to make on-site analysis. Back on earth, robots are used extensively to handle radioactive material, do work that requires great strength, and work with toxic materials too dangerous for humans. They can also do repetitive tasks that humans would find boring. But is such work an enhancement of man or his replacement? The answer is probably both. Surveys are predicting by 1990 100,000 to 200,000 American manufacturing jobs will disappear because of robots. **Fortunately**, over half of those displaced workers will have jobs working with the robots (within their present company.) **Unfortunately** these machines will now tell the workers what to do.

The computerization of the workplace is fundamentally different from previous forms of automation. The microchip symbolizes a far more powerful and pervasive technology than any encountered before. It not only reorganizes specific jobs, but how factories, corporations, and entire nations are run.

Japan is in the forefront of world technological development. There are half a million robots at work throughout the world today and Japan controls nearly 50 percent of all robotics manufacturing. Some are even programmed to build other robots—with only a few humans to supervise and help. One Japanese worker we talked with said that his "hands could cry" when robotics devices took over the skills that had taken him years to learn. Totally self-reproducing computer programs and small machines that can copy themselves are now reality. The Japanese, as part of their effort to become inventors as well as master duplicators, use about 30,000 of them in manufacturing everything from television sets to cameras.

In the United States, industry is drawing on three research centers for new applications of artificial intelligence and robotics. Carnegie-Mellon University, the Massachusetts Institute of Technology, and Stanford University. In addition to welders and painters, Stanford's laboratory has developed robot arms and legs for paraplegics as well as sight devices that are planted in the head to help the visually impaired "see."

We are just getting to a stage where we can use very largescale integrated circuit systems (VLSI) which will allow us to improve robots by as much as a thousand times. This will give them many of our sensory possibilities, the ability to analyze voices, billions of visual points, and sense the other characteristics of the real world. This whole area requires philosophers, sociologists, economists, artists, psychologists, and educators as well as engineers.

Simple robots have already explored various planets and part of the solar system. They have moved around on Mars, sampled the soil, and sent information and pictures back to earth. But these technological marvels often die unnatural deaths—sometimes by their former admirers. For example: an unused launching complex at Cape Canaveral with all of its automated robotics equipment now bears this notice. "Abandon in place, no further maintenance authorized." Similar notices are appearing on nuclear power plants and their robots (used to handle radioactive material). Living creatures, it seems, aren't the only things to "die."

Since robots can be programmed to replicate themselves, using only the raw materials available wherever they are, the possibilities in space exploration are endless. Science fiction books, like the children's book **The Space Visitor** (Dennis Adams), have covered some of this ground by constructing stories about self-replicating factories in space where generation after generation of machines toil away—using solar energy and local materials to replicate themselves and make a hospitable home for later arriving human expeditions. Just as science fiction writers look to technology and science for inspiration, science occasionally looks to science fiction for hints. Scientists at the Nuclear Weapons Laboratory, for example, report getting an idea for a robot detonated nuclear (explosion) powered laser from such literature.

Computer-controlled robots are everywhere. Some are real, others only give the illusion of robotics. Both have invaded children's toy boxes and television. Even the robot toys themselves often become television characters (**He-man** and **She-Ra**). Some children are introduced to "robots" through television programming that features them, as in **Masters of the Universe** or **Voltron**. Others learn of robots through the toys they are given. The **Omnibot 200** (by TOMY Corporation) and **Transformer** (Hasbro Bradley) are just two examples of children's toys that manufacturers call **robots**—yet they exhibit few characteristics of true robotics. Toy manufacturers, advertisements, store displays and publicity events pass these toys off as "robots." Coleco Industries (which lost money on microcomputers and gained it back with **Cabbage Patch** dolls) touches on the computer-based biotechnology revolution with robot toys (**Sectaurs**) that are insect-like humans that "resulted from a genetics experiment."

Coleco even has a **Rambo** (called **Dumbo** in England) robot doll. It is based on the very violet R-rated movie character protrayed by Sylvester Stallone. Coleco paraphrases President Regan's comment about the character, "...an emerging American hero...a justice seeking individual whose values and characteristics we all want..." The company adds "the dolls that reflect these values are the ones that we should want our children to play with." But as a third grader who had seen the ad said, "Rambo is the kind of toy you put batteries in and watch it kill Ken and Barbie." And it was the experience gained from using computers that helped open the door to initial viewing skills.

Psychologists are hired by advising companies on how to provide information to advertisers about how to attract children to particular toys.

Fortunately, at least some children with good critical thinking skills are able to separate the reality from the advertising image, and, more importantly, right from wrong. Let's hope that educators can do as good a job of sorting out the reality from the image—and the right from the wrong—when it comes to educational computing.

THE IMAGE VS. THE REALITY OF COMPUTERS IN THE SCHOOLS

Computer-based technological innovation is not simply sentimental background music for educational reform. It has a crucial role to play in the process. The problems lie in blowing the importance of educational computing all out of proportion and warping instructional reality; caused when educational policy is influenced by the masterfully filtered image of the new technology.

The selective attention of the media, combined with technological romanticism and vested commercial interests, brings about a coersive social-educational force that places instructional computing on the level of gospel (or at least a parable). Computers epitomize a promiscuous embrace of what's trendy and new. People don't know why they need a computer—but they fear life without one. The result is that a blind spot is created in our collective awareness. Any unpleasant educational computing realities are surpressed. This, in turn, gets in the way of deciding how, when, and especially IF, computers can be usefully employed in particular learning environments.

As educational computing has built a powerful constituency, it has become increasing difficult to take an adversative position. Computers may or may not help us invigorate the schooling process, but one thing is certain—stepping back and asking if computers really do amplify learning has become an increasingly unpopular role to play. Yet, the primary purpose is not to condemn, but to understand, clarify and place educational computing in perspective.

Is It Possible to Predict the Future by Inventing It?

With little debate, rhyme, or reason computers are being defused through the schools of the nation. In spite of this new reality, the educational future, either with or without computers, has yet to be decided. We can be certain, however, that the future is not simply an enlarged present—and only a few are clever enough to get close to predicting the future by inventing it. As accurate a past technological prognosticator as Jules Verne speculated that social institutions (including education) would continue along Victorian lines into the future. In this century both Edison and Bell thought that the telephone would be used by children (and adults) to listen to distant musical concerts. They also reasoned that the phonograph would be used to convey messages between distant groups in a way that would be excellent for school social studies programs. When radio, and later television, came along, both were viewed (by later day commentators) as potential saviors of mass education.

The only certainty is that some new technology does make a difference and that the social and educational implications are difficult, if not impossible, to predict. For educational computers, or any other technological innovation, there are a multitude of alternative futures. These become increasingly difficult to predict when the problem of anticipation becomes obscured by blatant boosterism. Collective enthusiasm (which seems to dim awareness) is no substitute for sound educational policy.

The Ideology of the Technological Fix

The social ideology of there being a futuristic technological fix for all of our problems—including those of the educational variety—seems to assume that the development of anything technological is desirable. This carries with it the implicit assumption that any technology should be immediately used simply because it is possible to do so.

Concerns with the values contained within—and carried by—computer based educational technology are brushed aside in our rush to be viewed as current. The simple truth is that there are technological solutions to only **some** educational problems. After all, as George Bernard Shaw said, "There is the wisdom of the head and the wisdom of the heart." In the future, as in the past, it will be human rather than mechanistic forces that will be most important in shaping learning experiences.

In teaching children to swim in future seas of information, we need all the human and non-human help that we can get. If computers can lend a hand in that adventure then they are welcome. But we must confuse neither the worshipping of technology nor the selling of microcomputers with the education of children.

Computing Before Culture

Computing time can diminish time spent with the humanities. When computers start being used by students, the result is a displacement of time and effort spent on other activities. And the activities first to go are those that are most experiential—painting, creative drama, movement and literature. In the schools examined in a recent pilot study, this meant less time for the humanities. And students who used computers at home spent less time either in athletic activities or reading books outside of the classroom. Computers also tended to raise new discriminatory barriers between the young and old, boys and girls, the more wealthy (who had them) and the less wealthy (who didn't). When computers are used by children, the time displacement is similar to what happens when television is viewed to exclusivity.

Both computers and television, especially when they are used together, can enable remote audiences to communicate. But as the research on instructional television suggests, the audience itself can remain remote in spirit. The one certain advantage is when students can see or interact with something that they might not experience in real life (such as views from the space shuttle). But all too often the artificial world presented by television, and now computers, replaces real experiences that are readily available.

To a degree the use of computers and their interconnection through networks can actually create, rather than reduce, barriers to inter/intrapersonal communication. The so-called "hacker" culture seems to isolate those who use computers from those who lack either the required learning style or the interest for dealing with the new technology. Questions of social isolation, equity, and the massive cost of "computer literacy" training (for both teachers and students are usually avoided in the educational literature.

The Growth of Computer Use in School Has Outstripped Educational Theory

Besides having little time on the potentially frustrating machine, computer breakdowns are often beyond a student's control. In contrast, when he is reading a book the page never goes blank—or when writing a story there is always the paper that keeps the words in place, with no loss of text if the electricity fails. With paper and pencil there are no error messages and if the pencil breaks it can be sharpened. Even the automatic assumption that the computer can improve writing skills has yet to come out in the educational research.

Of course computer technology is changing so rapidly that many current problems may be overcome. The real danger is allowing tendency towards technological self-deception to further remove children from real-world experiences.

The Commercial Promotion of Educational Computing

Computer companies, publishers selling educational software, and universities who want to sell teacher retraining courses, have done an excellent job of commercially promoting computers in the schools. Uncritical newspaper and journal coverage has also given educational computing a free ride. Some, like the various computer and technology magazines, even have editorial prohibition **against** articles that might cast the notion of children using computers in a bad light. Information that makes such a social force uneasy is quickly thrown into disrepute. In fact, many magazines have gone so far as to deny the existence of serious critics.

The use of computers in education has a long and questionable past and present. Few people have asked the basic questions about costs and benefits—or how both are distributed. Some of this disinformation even obscures the real causes of poor quality in education.

There are some basic critical questions that must be asked about the impact of technology that is being brought into the schools:

I. Do they amplify or diminish the acquisition of the very intellectual tools (skills) that are most useful in ordering the human mind—and essential for setting it free?

II. Are computers viewed as "the" answer to our national problems in education?

III. Are they used as a substitute for real people or things?

IV. Does the computer program allow for the expression and growth of feelings and values?

V. Is linear computer programming set up as a model for "good thinking?"

VI. Are the limitations of computers explained to children?

The degree to which we limit the debate about effective teaching and learning is the degree to which we limit choices and constrict the range of educational action.

The Role of the Teacher

In its beginning stage (1982-84), the use of computers in the schools seemed to primarily amplify existing teaching-learning methodologies and circumstances. Rather than revolutionizing the process, computers were most frequently used to convey some of the more conventional aspects of the present curriculum yet another step removed from reality. If the school curriculum is as mediocre as the recent rash of national reports suggests, then computers simply amplify mediocrity and provide us with more of what isn't working and in the process, trapping children in an even more artificial learning environment.

The educational impact of computers is only partially determined by computer hardware, software and societal popularity. Central to its use is how educators conceptualize the computer using process. In the final analysis, it is the teacher who must decide if, when, and how computers will be part of the instructional enterprise. It just may be the classroom teacher who first comes face to face with the realization that we can lull ourselves into a technological sleep. And it is the teacher (who must deal with the day-in, day-out issues of teaching and learning) who will be the first to re-examine learning realities as a result of computers being brought into the classroom. The computer may, after all the critics are through, be the catalyst for re-examining the very process of human learning itself. By having microcomputer programs in the schools, we are being forced to examine the classroom work that many had, either explicity or implicitly (correctly or incorrectly), assumed to work. Whatever the elements of reality and illusion, if the appearance of microcomputers results in nothing more than causing us to examine what we are teaching (and why we are teaching it) then it will indeed have played a critical role in educational reform. **The history of both technology and pedagogy are full of polarizations, reversals, and contradictions.** [Dennis Adams, conference paper, 1984].

TELLING THE REAL FROM THE UNREAL: COMPUTER-CONTROLLED IMAGES AND LEARNING

In 1984 we saw the first signs of a serious backlash against educational computing. Hardware couldn't solve all of our educational problems. We had finally reached a point where people began to rebel against the euphoric hype (surrounding microcomputers) that had been going on unabated for three or four years. Journalists, with an educational background, would review a piece of drill and practice software and decide that educational computing was limited and that a workbook would be better. The major criticism centered around the notion that the computer-based technology might replace real experience—or even real people—in the classroom. In some cases this had happened; instead of using more expensive science equipment, some schools were saving money by limiting students to manipulating objects and chemicals on the screen. Others figured that since others had computers, they could up the student to faculty ratio. Still, in spite of some misuse of technology, the criticism that electronic experiences were replacing **real** experiences on a massive scale was unfounded. Do children **have** to touch something before it becomes real? Images can, after all, be powerful realities.

After a period of computer bashing, the time may now be ripe for a swing back towards moderation. Of course serious criticism and educational computing need each other. But those of us who are writing critical and cautionary articles about how microcomputers and television trap children in artificial worlds have more than made our point. Microcomputers, videodiscs and VCRs are a fact of life and are having an impact on how we formulate our perception of what's real. Reality itself is changing as rapidly as the technology defining it. Certainly some skepticism and concern is healthy, but exaggeration can kill a new instructional tool before it has a chance to reach its potential. This is particularly true now that a technological synthesis is on the immediate horizon—with a kind of electronic synergism about to take place.

Actual Experience is Not the Only Connection to Reality

Just as science frequently confuses fact with truth, educators frequently confuse what's found in the physical (non-electronic) environment with what's most real for the child. If it's machine-assisted, it must be mechanized and less valuable than actual (real) experience. The truth is that sometimes it is, and sometimes it isn't. There are limits to actual experience. Intellectual enrichment can come from any direction that stimulates the brain with novelty and challenge. Certainly we want children painting with real brushes—but that doesn't negate the learning experience that can come from doing art on the computer because that too can become part of the "real world."

The form and style of reality is changing. When children use a computer hooked up to a videodisc—or other television media—they can tour an art museum in any way they want, viewing the art from any angle, even calling up printed text information if they like. The force and clarity of this visually based learning should not be underestimated.

The reality of human learning is that there are a vast range of different styles in thinking and learning. And adding a computer-based technology to the mix has the potential of opening up avenues for a wider range of intelligences than traditional methods. Of course, the manner in which children come across ideas will affect their use. But intelligently programmed electronic devices would seem to only add to the possibilities—discovery **can** take place in both new and old ways. Even the primitive, non-interactive television technology that we have with us now can be intelligently and critically viewed and used educationally. In spite of all its present limitations, it does give us the very first information about what's going on in the real world. And some of what it presents is simply not something that we can experience in our daily lives. Better programming and merger with other media could really change our conception of the medium. Despite the disappointment that the microcomputer cannot solve all of our instructional problems, new windows are being opened.

While it's true learning is powerfully affected by experience, some actual life experiences are not experiential. The abstract "unreal" is, at least occasionally, the most "real." Actual experience is only one way to approach understanding reality. We can, for example, have experience in our heads—or with computer controlled simulations. Like a book, or any other curriculum material, these can be used as jumping off points for the exploration of the limitations of our "real world" models. And, as the technology develops, these electronic excursions will themselves become more and more real.

Real world lessons do not automatically hold any more true and internal (what goes on in our minds) or external (electronic) lessons. The field and the streets are not necessarily more accurate in teaching perceptual truths than our minds or our video screens. You can be tricked by the real world as easily as the electronic one. There are multiple ways of arriving at the "truth." In fact, internal critical thinking skills and external computer controlled video technology can help us balance out some of the illusions thrown at us from our physical environment. There is **some** truth to the expression "seeing is believing." And technology can help us "see" things that would otherwise not be part of our reality. We can see reality with electronics that we could not see in the real world; building graphic models to represent DNA molecules is one example.

Technology can also stimulate an enriched learning environment, helping us bring distant or uncommon events into our consciousness and change our view of reality. Interacting with historical events and atomic reactors would be impossible in real life. Yet, these and other events can enter our personal realities with computer-based technology. But be careful, magazines (including the **National Geographic**) and newspapers frequently use computers to alter almost anything they want in a picture. The camera simply puts the picture onto the TV screen and a computer allows the editor to rearrange any of the elements. The pyramids, for example, were digitized and rearranged to "fit" on the cover of **National Geographic**. Although prohibitively expensive today, it is possible to do the same thing with film; transplanting a moving character from an old to a new movie or television segment. These electronic experiences—along with the internal mental sorting and evaluating—may be distant from concrete material but they will be just as real.

Some symbolic and analytical thinking may not even be possible in our physical environment. Certainly, experience of all kinds and dimensions influences the ongoing narrative in our heads. When we can mix the internal thinking process with electronic devices **and** concrete material, then we have the most powerful learning combination. In the immediate future, the widespread use of computer-linked video equipment will provide realistic sight, sound, movement, and interaction—making it an even more powerful part of the thinking learning process. Computer controlled devices (as with the books that they are starting to replace) can help us experience the abstract, the symbolic, and the real.

When real world experience with actual material is a possibility, it should take place. Technology should be viewed as a supplement or amplification, not as a replacement. But when actual experience is impossible, the mechanical devices and internal thinking processes can help us build—and take apart—representations of real world models. Computer controlled technology can help students understand the relationship between elements and the limitations of the models we use to represent them. Television, particularly when linked to a computer, changes the limits of real time and space in ways that allow us to view both differently. Even in reality, scientific models are more like simulations than perfect representations of real world experience—and the better we understand that, the better we understand the underlying process. Technology can help us explore the complexity of such models in a more graphic, concrete and visual manner than is possible by mathematical formula or the printed word.

Figure 3. Digitized photograph of Roger Brown's painting **Seeking Shelter**.

Educational Computing: Self-Satisfaction or Criticism?

When educational computing was just beginning to get moving (only 4 or 5 years ago), it generated too much self-satisfaction—followed by too much criticism. Exaggeration in either direction can prevent the integration of a new learning process. Progress requires a little skepticism and a little faith. But the critic who says that computers in education will fare no better than some previous technologies (like programmed learning and educational television) should remember that we only have an average of one computer for every fifty children in school. (In poorer districts it is one for every seventy.) Dismissing such devices now is a little like dismissing books in 1780. After all, they didn't help much—and with an average of one per class what came out of primitive printing presses didn't seem as lively (or as real) as those done by hand.

Programmed learning and educational television failed to treat the child as a thinking and contributing individual. The computer is assuming a new role, encouraging children to accept a greater amount of responsibility for their own learning process. Seeing the future of educational computing is a little like trying to envision a 747 while watching the Wright Brothers. Those who are very self-satisfied about the present stage of computers in the schools and have accepted the computer as the answer for most of our educational ills are making the same mistake as the critics. Fanaticism or extreme claims can cloud the picture and make everything more difficult for a rapidly changing educational technology. The overly enthusiastic and the overcritical might best be served by a middle course of moderation. If expectations in either direction are too grand, then disillusionment is bound to set in and a powerful learning tool will either fall short of its potential or be lost altogether.

Connecting Everything to Everything

While we are arguing the specifics of early 80s computing, the world is turning and many of these factors are already prehistoric distractions. Today's technology allows cellular mobile phone systems to use computer controlled networks of radio transmitters to route data and calls to and from mobile phones (often in cars) or computer-based databases. Even new computer chip technology has reached a stage where it is possible to process information in almost any frequency—from the human voice to computers, to television and beyond. When these microchips are put into civilian action, it will be possible to use computer technology to control television sets, personal computers, radios, and other electronic devices connecting everything to the human voice or anything else found in the frequencies of nature.

IBM and AT&T are just two of the larger companies (to say nothing of the Defense Department) that have recognized the possibilities in these breakthrough technologies. (Witness IBM's recent alliance with MCI communications and CBS.) IBM, Texas Instruments, Honeywell, Motorola, Hughs, Westinghouse, and National Semiconductor are the major firms working on these very high speed integrated circuits (VHSIC chips). These new chips support the evolution of computer-based electronic systems—with great increases in speed, accuracy, picture clarity, and instant connection to just about any sound or picture that is desired. TV pictures can be stored in computer memories, pictures from several sources can be pulled onto a screen with freeze frames and close ups and even a printed text explanation. The learning possibilities are endless.

At the same time as we are coming up with more powerful learning microworlds, we are getting closer to being an electronic village on a world-wide scale. The time is rapidly approaching when computer controlled technology will make it possible for just about anybody with the proper (inexpensive) computer controlled devices to communicate with anything any place else in a multitude of ways. A form of computer-based video may be the key technology for providing alternative paths for learning. The real concern is with the quality spectrum the medium will be programmed to carry in the future—rather than old criticisms about trapping children in artificial worlds.

Animated video microworlds can be built by children to explore concepts from literature to mathematics. But as far as present day broadcast television is concerned, the idea of searching for truth, as opposed to just presenting a version of it, is something that remains in the future. But today's TV is the thin edge of the wedge that is opening up new experiential forms and styles. Interactive cable television and computer/video communication links will allow for learning options undreamt of in 1985. Everything from the home to the world will be electronically brought into the process—allowing us to use the media to chase and explore interacting images.

Computers can allow the child and the technology to work purposefully together without isolation from the important classroom activities. Observation of groups of children interacting with computer activities suggests that the level of cooperation is higher than the behavior of the same children engaged in other activities. It may well be that given computer-based group interaction and choices helps children learn about personal and group responsibility and interpersonal relations in the larger world. Giving pupils a choice and a certain level of independence is better training for the real world than teaching by rote, but this can turn to educational chaos under mediocre teachers. Both teachers and students will be presented with more and more choices; therefore, the importance of intelligent decision-making, in an ambiguous world, will dramatically increase.

Virtually all telecommunications have been created or processed by some sort of computer. These communication devices (mainly television at the moment) have enormous intrusive, reality forming power. Witness last year's hijacking of an airline by terrorists who literally shot themselves into every living room. One jarring moment was when the ABC anchorman (on "Good Morning America") turned to Cory Aquino in the Philippines and said, "Any final words to President Reagan this morning?" (The American president reportedly had the TV on in his bedroom.) Even in today's limited format, TV messages can be conveyed to both leader and massive publics of billions around the globe.

The Live Aid (for Africa) concert is another example of how computer controlled video can participate in a global human intellectual and social revolution. It went out to more than fifty countries. Concert lighting (VariLite) was made possible by computer controls preprogrammed and saved on disks. The sound systems were similarly customized (by Ultra Sound) and the instruments themselves were programmed with precise mathematical accuracy. There were musicians from England, the USA, Australia, Ireland, the Soviet Union and other countries—all working for free. Of course, some of the best moments were missed by the TV networks going to laxative and pimple cream commercials in the middle of songs. The message was essentially healthy, in spite of the greed on the part of the commercial networks and coverage by announcers who might most charitably be described as mindless adolescents. However, the potential of television for doing positive things should not be missed. Of course, it was aimed more at the emotional eye than the analytic mind, but it is proving that people can communicate with machines and with other people.

No matter how real or how healthy, conventional television usually shows a few of the facts, but misses the truth. And as it can make complex distant events immediate and concrete, it can also be dangerous. It can put terrorists in our living room or positively mix commercial greed, music and food for starving people. Reality, illusion, or a mix of both can be conveyed to the viewer. When it opens its lenses for a mass audience, TV can even change the essential nature of the event it conveys. The images that television transmits may carry more power than the reality of what's in that image. This is even evident in what's censored out of our reality. The BBC, for example, was recently accused by a Labor Member of Parliament as acting as "thought police" for not broadcasting a program on the IRA. Prime Minister Margaret Thatcher, on the other hand, was very pleased that they didn't "further the objectives of IRA terrorists." Censorship or a high level of social responsibility? Take your pick.

Irregardless of the politics involved, a powerful synergism is emerging from speeding up the interaction of ideas, learning and technology. IBM and Elk Industries have developed a technology called **Phonemail** that allows a series of **electronic mailboxes** to receive, store, and transmit both visual and voice messages. **Tektronic** and **Knowledge Systems Inc.** are just two of the companies offering information management software that allows users to skip between messages—following a particular theme or idea. People need help in learning how to sift the popular image of what's real from the underlying reality. The common sense knowledge surrounding what's viewed on the street, whether in Beirut, Washington, or Greeley, may be less real than a careful analysis of the medium, symbols and the sequence in which ideas are presented. Just as the technology can keep people away from meaning, it can also help people come closer to it. Productive thought can be amplified or diminished through a combined play of images and symbols. Computer-controlled world communications can also help people get direct experience with formal systems, symbols, and meaning behind what's in the environment. Computer-based technology can also help us keep track of the dramatic potential in our growing number of options and learning style choices.

As the technology advances, so will the need to reexamine our humanity. Even the present primitive versions of electronic pipelines show how a focus on the humanities may be the most human of networking. (Two recent examples are the Aid [for Africa] concerts and US Festival.) One of the best producers of programming that stimulates thinking is the **Public Broadcasting System**. Unfortunately, PBS is having its funding cut drastically—clouding its future. Enriching the lives of viewers is only a bright promise that challenges the rest of the communications world to use TV better.

The very existence of the technology (good or bad) causes us to reexamine our human qualities—thus the humanities are natural focuses. Putting culture and human experience first leaves plenty of room in our schools for the computer-based amplification of learning.

Technology is so much a part of what we define as real that the critics who say that when it's used in instruction it prevents students from getting at the real world, miss the point. Reality is changing as rapidly as video images and computing. And there is no turning back of the clock. We might as well make the best of it by improving the programming and teaching our students how to think critically about these electronic devices and the messages they carry.

It **is** possible to use computer controlled technology to explore the complexity of reality; rather than the educational equivalent of the simplified headlines seen on the network news. Teaching critical viewing skills and using interactive computers can help us to deal with the disguises, exaggerations and artificial universe implicit in the technology. The whole process will require new styles of critical thinking, viewing and being on the user's part. With the video screen becoming the most common purveyor of information, **visual fluency** is an essential skill.

By teaching critical viewing skills and enlisting the technology itself in the effort, we can help the mass media to grow out of its present mischievous adolescence. With electronic communications moving inexorably forward, it is time for television/computer democracies to grow up before the next electronic onslaught begins. Computerized data bases, viewed with video screens, already contain the microchip equivalent of thousands of print and pictoral libraries.

As diverse mediums (including personal computers and television) are giving common connecting points on a world-wide basis, the potential for good or evil, real or unreal, experiential or artificial, are all present. Critical thinking and viewing skills will become increasingly important as computers allow us to digitize almost any image and put it into action reality. There is no way to legislate against our rapidly evolving electronic mediums. They are as real as anything that children can touch. We have to assist the various mediums in the growing process. And the schools have the responsibility of giving children some skill in sifting through the messages. If our educational system is to play its part in the process, then it must not only provide alternative means of thinking about and exploring curriculum topics, but reconceptualize its view of reality and experience. Certainly the best way to learn is through experience. But in light of our evolving electronic miracles, we not only must reconceptualize teaching and learning but what "experience" means in the interplay of ideas and machines. The process itself is enormously diverse with basic truths presenting themselves in many guises. Computers seem to provide a catalyst for educational choices and are becoming part of the most powerful learning technology ever developed. But programming and "computer literacy" (as we know it today) may very well fade from the scene.

As antiquated equipment is replaced, some elements of educational computing philosophy may become stronger than ever. The notion of discovery by choice—and user control—behind some of the elements of today's educational computing will almost certainly carry over into a new age; an age where activities in the mind and experience with electronic devices will be considered as legitimate an experience and as "real" as what's picked up in the physical environment.

Computerized word processing and the challenges of interactive fiction have already transformed major elements of human creativity. Computer-controlled electronic elements are rapidly becoming a primary means of creating the world of experience and ideas in the future—in fact, they will be central to thinking, learning and communicating. As technologies emerge and integrate so do traditional divided human skills. We are in the process of major transformations in how knowledge is acquired and communicated. Our range of choices are being dramatically increased by the unique creative momentum that educational computing continues to generate. As new technological combinations collect, analyze, and deliver information, it is creating new tasks. Our society must decide for itself if it wants the kind of access to the world of ideas and enlightened learning that the technology can help give us. It is now time to stop attacking the old (early 80s) computer technology and assume responsibility for how the reality of our future is being created through ideas—experiential, internal and electronic. After all, it just may be one of the keys to developing a society that allows each person the opportunity to fulfill his or her unique aspirations.

Figure 4. Computer Composite Image.

THE FUTURE: A FIFTH GENERATION OF COMPUTERS

The first generation of computers was based on the technology of an electronic vacuum tube; the second, a small vacuum tube; the third, a transistor. The fourth, an integrated circuit, depends on a tiny silicon chip to store and process information that once required warehouses of storage room. The fifth generation will feature artificially intelligent machines that can **produce**, as well as process, information. Such computers actually make judgments and draw conclusions about input data. Beyond 1990 living cell protein, bacteria cell level in size, may be used much like a silicon microchip is used today.

In keeping with its cultural concern with adapting to new circumstances, and convinced that thinking machines are the real power of the future, the Japanese government launched a major research effort on artificial intelligence in 1981. This project has long-term research and development financing coupled to long-term marketing and sales strategies. In the United States, the private sector responded with a less ambiguous project—over a dozen companies joined to form the Microelectronics and Computer-Technology Corporation (MCC) in 1982. MCC member companies include Advanced Micro Devices, Allied Control Data, Digital Equipment, Harris, Honeywell, Martin Marietta, Motek, Motorola, National Cash Register, National Semiconductor, RCA, and Sperry Univac. Based in Austin, Texas, and headed by Admiral Bobby Ray Inman (former head of the CIA), MCC has impressive resources, but there is a certain reluctance to invest in long-term research and development on the part of the American companies. In addition, U.S. researchers are playing a catch-up game with their Japanese counterparts. Private companies (in their fierce races with one another to bring products to market) and Defense Department research have stifled traditionally open exchange among researchers. This can seriously impede new research which, in turn, could hamper our national development of fifth generation computers that will influence everything from creative expression to geopolitics—and as a consequence, deserves treatment as a strategic commodity. After all, the semiconductors that run this technology will be the foundation of all of electronics—transforming our lives as they control computers, telecommunications, artificial intelligence, energy-technology and weaponry.

Already Japanese machine-knowledge engineers are experimenting with a book-sized reading device that uses silicon chips, each containing the contents of several books. Adding "expert systems" to these could make use of a teacher's knowledge to go from written word to sound or a discussion depending on how a particular student learns best. Replicating certain functions associated with human intelligence allows these artificially intelligent machines to improve their work as a result of experience or electronic learning.

In the United States, scientists at Dartmouth University have recently put the entire contents of the **Encyclopedia Britannica** on three videodiscs, each side containing 52,000 pages. Using an Apple IIe microcomputer and about $600 worth of additional equipment—a videodisc player and connecting link—you can go from page 1 to page 35,000 in a couple seconds. With today's first-generation microcomputer (part of the fourth generation of computers), we can use color, video, high-resolution graphics, sound, animation, and speech synthesis and still have the capacity to rapidly manipulate enormous amounts of data. Linking today's microcomputers to telecommunications allows us to transmit pictures or data the same way we broadcast television signals. The process is called teleprocessing and gives us the means to rapidly link computers through the air.

By looking back to biology, we may even be able to look beyond fifth generation computers. Scientists are now considering a radically different kind of computer that is based on molecular reactions of living cells rather than silicon. Bacteria have used sophisticated chemical processes to transfer information for billions of years. Their enzymes work by stereoscopically matching their molecules with other molecules, a decision making process that occurs more than 10,000 times a second. Using this model of biological functioning, it may be possible to build a computer that is half alive/half electronics cell.

Computer controlled combinant DNA technology is launching us on a voyage with social side effects even more exotic than our adventure with the silicon microchip. Cell functions can be taken from particular species (including germs and viruses) and relocated where they are most useful or profitable. These new developments may result in networks of "biochips" which can be bred by the millions and put to work in knowledge processing. Why? Because digital computers may have a limited potential for simulating thought, and there are styles of problem solving that may not be digitally computable. Biological science mechanisms may advance "computing" as the research curves in both areas cross. Our society is paying for the work and has a right to some control over the direction of the work—and a right to most of the benefits.

In the future we may see a different style of computing—less rigid and working more like a brain than a machine. In fact, the mood of such a device might affect the way scientists solve problems. Figuring out what this will look like in the future is a little like trying to see the space shuttle when Goddard was experimenting with the first primitive rocket.

It is important to view both present and future advances as a **means** to communication; what the French call **telematique** (telematic society). When computer driven technology is viewed as a means rather than an end, people can use it to stretch their imaginations and increase the number of options which in itself is a kind of freedom. Combining dramatic changes in telecommunications, automation, and computing enable the storage and manipulation of vast amounts of knowledge. Like an exciting friend, computer controlled technology can invite us to do things that may not have even crossed our minds. Entering the new world of better access to information is very enticing, but computers also force us to ask some hard questions:

- How can we possibly handle this information onslaught?
- Is it more correct to say that we live in an information age or age of infoglut?
- Are we a process through which another form of intelligence is itself evolving?
- How much bioengineering must take place before something crosses the line of being human?
- What roles have, and will computers play in our world?
- Where is that literacy-intensive technology taking us and what are our options?
- What measure of control do we really have over the machines we create?
- Does **high tech** also bring high risk (genetic engineering, nuclear power, chemical plants, weaponry, etc.?
- How can we use our knowledge and influence to find out about computer applications that are good for society rather than harmful and dehumanizing?
- If the current generation of students is not as well educated as the last, how can the technology help us reverse that trend?
- Will our society provide schools with the means to make their contribution to shape the future?

The answers to these questions will be determined, in part, by how well we prepare this generation of students to work with the coming generations of computers.

CHAPTER 2

COMPUTERS ARE BASIC

JUST AS IT TOOK TIME for television to move beyond simply being visual radio to a unique medium, it has taken some time for computers to move beyond the rather boring scope of drill-and-practice and traditional workbook-like instruction. Computer-based technology offers unique potential for new forms of music composition, art, writing, reading, problem solving, experimentation and self expression. Whether using the computer as an electronic workbook, a language experience story, a science experiment, a four dimensional mathematical model, a tutor, or to enter the fantasy world of interactive children's literature, its potential as a powerful learning tool cannot be diminished.

It is difficult to ignore the presence of computers in education. A key is combining teaching methodology with computer enhancement. Not only are they being written about and discussed as an important frontier of modern thought and education, but with the tremendous influx of computers into the schools they are rapidly becoming a fact of classroom life. And we, as teachers, are emersed in the process of sorting out what uses we can and should make of this machine-based technology to amplify learning. As we move in the direction of enhancing human potential, we need to explore the computer as part of our cultural environment and learn how to best use it to reach our instructional objectives. In our effort to use the interactive capacities of a computer to their fullest, it is important to move beyond traditional instructional methods to viewing the machines as an object or tool with which to think and learn.

Computing: The New Basic Skill

Computers have entered our lives, our society, our thinking styles, even our ways of thinking about ourselves. Computer use has become so essential to our way of life that in 1983 the U.S. Department of Education recognized computing as a potential fourth basic skill. The term "computer literacy" has almost become a byword for instructional programs that teach about computers and how to integrate computer technology into our lives. How computers function, how we use and program them and how they impact society continues to be an important part of our modern curriculum.

Computer Awareness

Students need to be aware of how this new technological infusion is entering every aspect of their lives: from household appliances, to schools, stores, banks, offices, governmental services, law enforcement, health care, transportation, even the cable television service. Like it or not, computers have made a place for themselves in classrooms, libraries, work, art, music, sports, and entertainment.

As a subject of instruction, we need to look at the role of computers now, and in the future. With the convergence of research and development curves in computing, artificial intelligence, robotics, and molecular biology, many are confused. Others have raised concerns about how a new generation of computers will be controlled. The way we communicate with computers is already being greatly expanded. We will most likely exit the 1980s talking to computers rather than using keyboards. Beyond this, a system is being tested which allows severely handicapped people to communicate with machine intellligence by simply using their eyes. Eye movements instruct the computer to open or close the doors and windows, turn on or off the lights, televisions, radios, etc.

Researchers are already developing a computer communication system that uses an electroencephalogram (a device for measuring brainwaves). The user's brainwaves are compared with patterns programmed into the computer's memory. In the near future, computers may very well be an extension of the brain. One practical result might be classrooms wired for brainwave or voice control. If that seems too farfetched, remember that the new F-15 fighter plane has many controls under voice control to free the pilot's hands for other activities.

As computers come to pervade many aspects of our lives, it is important that school curriculum projects work beyond a narrow scope. If computer instruction is to succeed, it must be integrated across subject areas and focus on computer-based technology for all, not just for future

Figure 5. Computer Composite Image.

scientists or college bound students. Certainly no one group has a corner on the crucial computer concerns of sound reasoning and clear thought.

As a starting point, students need an appreciation of the background, capabilities and the limitations of the computer as well as a strong background in critical thinking, communication skills, the liberal arts, math and science. In Chapter 3, we will sample a variety of computer awareness activities to assist in the learning process.

COMPUTERS AND READING

Johnny can't compute because Johnny can't read or write. Computers and language skills cannot be separated. Reading on the computer is more than a novelty. Computers have the potential to alter the nature of traditional static print. The reader can rearrange the structure and contents of the printed text, actively participate in the story and call up parts of the text for further exploration. Readers may ask for descriptions of designated points, digress to related issues or speed through uninteresting or irrelevant material. This flexible computerized text presentation also allows for quick access to material. For example, one videodisc can store over 50,000 pages of the Encyclopedia Britannica, allowing a page of the reader's choice to be located and displayed in less than a second. Videodiscs can be **read** by computers just as they can read a floppy computer disk. Pictures and print data can be stored and accessed randomly; pulling an idea here, a picture there, as desired.

With or without videodisc players, computers have the unique capability of incorporating sequence, time, space, animation, indexing, and notetaking, making it a dynamic medium for reading instruction. It can modify, expand, collapse and reorganize the printed text. Students can call up specific topics by subject or headings, get assistance in vocabulary/pronunciation, and be provided with lists of synonyms. Online dictionaries make it possible for students to look up definitions without moving away from the video monitor. Additional reading tools such as an index, glossary, and thesaurus are also available to help readers comprehend difficult materials.

Speed is also a valuable advantage when reading on the computer. Computers can locate, sort and record information quickly. The reader of a science text, for example, could instruct the computer to display all information about volcanic eruptions since 1950. These multiple index terms, usually available in books, are time saving devices for readers and researchers. Information can also be individualized and cued; key words may be capitalized and information outlined or mapped from the text. Computers will even present notes on important issues and highlight important concepts. To increase comprehension or as an aid for slow readers, the print can be increased in size, the speed of the text can be altered and graphics added.

Computer-based reading presents new consequential reading possibilities. Every reader does not have to take the same route through the text. Some new microcomputer reading programs make it possible to call up specific packets of ideas in any order that interests the reader. Students can look at information on different levels with software programs like **Notecards**, described by its producer, the Xerox Corporation, as a **hypertext**. This type of program allows nonsequential connections to cross references and gives students the possibility of hopping from article to article following a given idea and allowing the user to follow any path on the story or concept roadmap.

Innovation in the presentation of print and graphics is also an advantage when using the computer for reading instruction. Pictures can be great communicators. Text can be arranged by thought units instead of in the conventional compact form. Colorful animated graphics make the text come alive. Students can slow down or speed up the action.

It is important to remember that good computer-based reading instruction incorporates both the principles of effective reading methodology and computer technology. Computer-based reading programs should be organized on an understanding of computers, foster active student involvement and focus on comprehension. Reading should not be taught as a collection of isolated skills; rather the emphasis should be placed on reading prose. Subskills should be placed within the context of meaningful reading. We must not allow our reading programs to be turned into techno-subskill dumps that obscure the beauty of literature and reading. It is crucial that computer-based reading activities be child centered and accommodate individual learning styles.

Just as we are concerned about the nature of reading **on** the computer, we should be concerned with reading **about** the computer. Questions should be raised as to whether or not these stories help readers understand the technology and its potential. The image of computer technology that enters the traditional medium of children's literature often reinforces societal stereotypes about science and technology. Who uses it, how it can be used to violate someone else's privacy, are all moral dilemmas that can be discussed at different levels as children are reading. Fortunately, they are often the first ones to spot misrepresentation of what computers can do, and the potential for their abuse. As teachers, we need to help them become critical consumers of this literature.

USING THE COMPUTER AS A PENCIL: WRITING AND COMMUNICATING WITH MACHINE INTELLIGENCE

The "computer as a pencil" metaphor brings home the message that our major communication tools are changing. "Writing on the computer is easier because it seems more like talking," remarked one fifth grader. And indeed it is. The computer responds to students, carries out their instructions, prompts them to keep to the point, checks for spelling mistakes and offers a communication channel for interacting with others, with the machine, and with themselves. Beyond the pencil/computer metaphor, the computer is bringing together thinking and writing in ways that the pencil, pen and typewriter never have. In **prewriting**, the computer can help children choose topics and plan their approach

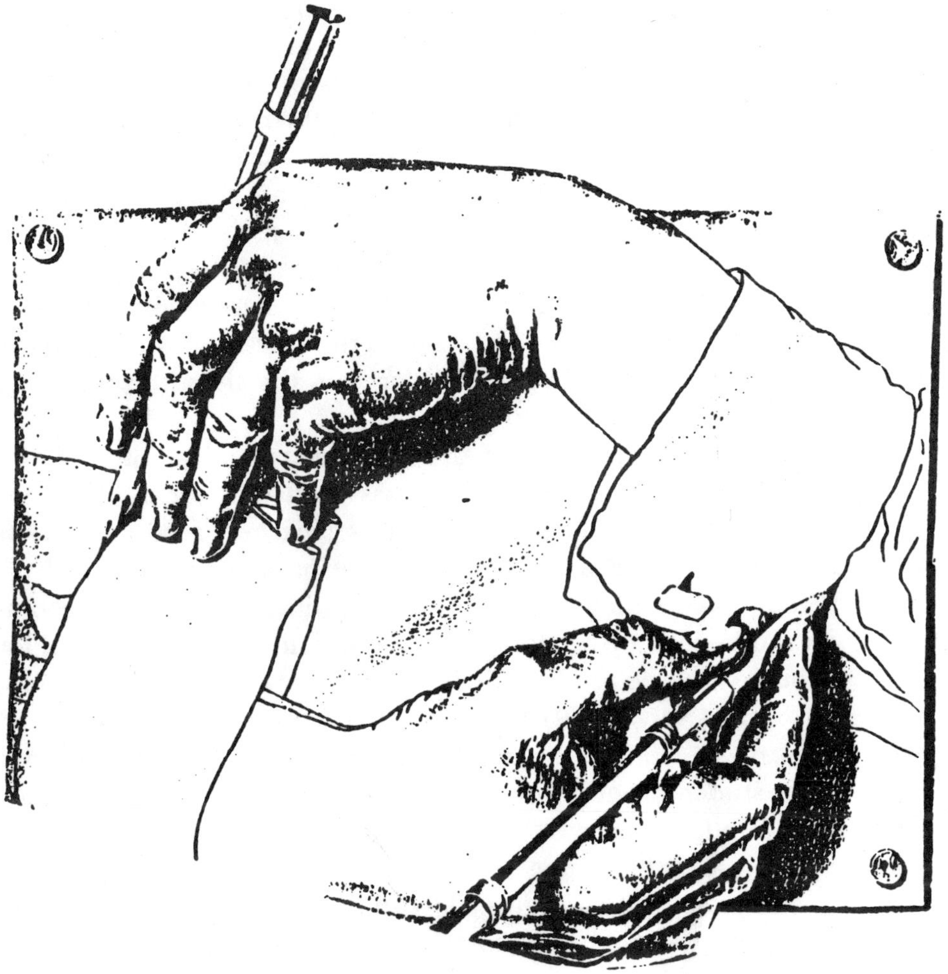

Figure 6. Computer as a Pencil Metaphor. Digitized photograph of an illustration by M.C. Escher.

through activities such as mapping. Students use a word processing program to do the actual writing, and in the postwriting phase even young children revise and rewrite.

Students find it easier to make the transition from speaking to writing because writing on the computer is interactive—an activity somewhere between talking and writing with a pencil. It is also highly motivating. When students use a word processing program, they are less bothered by mistakes or corrections and are more willing to revise their work. Words, sentences and paragraphs can be moved around and mistakes easily corrected. There is less resistance to reworking successive drafts. No more erasing until a hole appears in the paper.

After writing and revising, the child can join a small group of classmates, together they act as editors. Although the research suggests that process and meaning are more important than traditional rules, students at any age may run a rule centered program to check grammar, graphics and continuity. When editing is completed and graphics or illustrations added, the student pushes a button to run the printer and the writing appears **book perfect**. Software programs are available that allow for a variety of print styles and sizes. Writings can be bound, Dewey decimal numbers affixed, and books placed in the class library or sent home for families and friends to enjoy.

Writing is a tool for learning in all subject areas, and children writing on a computer tend to experiment across curricular areas. They put down more ideas and develop longer stories. Teachers report that word processing also has had a positive influence on students' research reports, fiction, poetry and letter writing along with language and reading skills. Reading skills of decoding, comprehension, sentence building, and vocabulary can be reinforced. It is easier for children to follow the notion of "what I can think I can say; what I can say, I can write" (or "someone can write for me"); and "what is written can be read by me and others." For students who dislike or cannot type, a peripheral device is available that allows them to print, or write in longhand, on a touch-sensitive plate; and the computer transfers it to the screen in typed format. New software programs also allow students to produce illuminated manuscripts in a scribe like style. Typefaces can be altered, margins moved in or out, and pages contracted or expanded (convenient for the sixth grader who must make a four page theme extend to five). The whole process gives children more opportunity to demonstrate what they have learned about writing.

Some teachers express concern over what the computer can and cannot do. Even though the computer is powerful, it is important to remember that the writer has to know what to say and how to say it. Many students have been missing the opportunity to step back and view the relationship between ideas. The computer is a valuable device for recording our thoughts—utilizing writing to discover and develop meaning. Computers can help us watch what we do with words, and help us understand what words do with us. Students seem to improve most when computer-based writing is combined with structured writing assignments and peer response groups—where specific questions and criteria was applied to the writing. Machine intelligence has provided us with an exciting new pencil and sketch pad that serves as a communication tool and an extension of the child.

THE COMPUTER AS A TOOL FOR TEACHING MATHEMATICS

The bulk of mathematics microcomputer software today is of the drill and practice variety. But mathematics is more than merely finding the right answer or "arriving" at a solution. It's a way of thinking, ordering and reasoning. Students in our mathematics classes often hand in assignments devoid of any serious analysis or relationships. Part of the problem is that mathematicians deal in abstractions which many students are not developmentally able to handle. Often, too, children fail to see the connection of mathematics to their lives and incorporate concepts in a meaningful way. The computer can be used as a powerful tool to enhance understanding and serve as a bridge between concrete and abstract concepts.

Using Logo programs, for example, students can explore and discover mathematical relationships, solve problems and reinforce concepts.[1] It is important to develop activities and projects that encourage students to actively explore topics, make use of problem solving, procedural and critical thinking skills. For conceptual development to occur, students need a variety of learning experiences both on and off the computer. Computers can be used in pre and post math activities—as well as in the heart of the lesson itself. Experimental and manipulative materials should not be replaced. They can be mixed with actual work on the computer or precede it. One way to do a lesson is to use a guided discovery approach including the following elements:

Precomputer Lesson
Guided Discovery with Computers
Follow-up Computer Activity
Extended Learning Activity

Precomputer activities can introduce and set the stage for developing mathematics concepts off the computer. Concrete manipulatives like base ten blocks, balance and weights, attribute blocks, cuisianaire rods,

[1] Clarke, V.A. and Chambers, S.M. **Thinking with Logo: Apple version**. Sydney, McGraw Hill, 1985.

and geoboards allow students to discover relationships and learn about concepts first hand before moving to graphic computer simulations. Students generate hypotheses based on actual hands on manipulation of materials and amplify these experiences with the computer.

Guided discovery computer activities gives students hand-on experience in an environment which encourages exploration. Hypotheses are able to be tested and students experiment beyond, as one idea triggers another. In Logo, children can create visual models incorporating the concepts introduced, test these concepts in new situations and explore further. In simplified contexts, for example, students may employ knowledge of coordinate grids to help place the Logo turtle in different positions. Exploring initially with geoboards and graph paper, students get a feel for the coordinate system in precomputer activities before moving to the Logo environment. Once in the world of the turtle, children can experiment by plotting points and manuevering the turtle, creating their own visual models—reinforcing and extending the concepts introduced.

Follow up computer activities are an essential part of the mathematics lesson. Students need opportunities to present and discuss their findings, review and strengthen mathematical ideas they have experimented with. Verbalizing relationships discovered and explored on the computer illuminates student meanings and interpretations. It also affords opportunities for generating conclusions and making generalizations.

Logo is not the only route to learning mathematics on the computer. As with any good lesson, the teacher needs to offer suggestions for further exploration and generate possible activities for questions to **extend the topic**. It is important for computer activities to be tied to higher order thinking skills and problem solving. Questioning techniques and problem posing are key strategies for the computer using teacher.

There are a number of ways to make the computer a valuable tool for actively involving students in the learning process. Children tend to solve problems in informal ways despite exposure to formal methods. Using the technology as a discovery tool builds connections between spontaneous mathematics and "traditional" mathematics curriculums. By tapping microcomputers into international networks, students can look at how children in other countries use measurement, numeration, games, and mathematics in their daily lives. The same high technology that holds the key to our destruction also holds the key to our survival.

Creative Problem Solving

Unlike the syntactical structure of art, mathematics is structured on rules which must be followed. And many do not perceive mathematics as a creative endeavor because often it does not provide opportunities for students to formulate unique solutions or create uniquely productive work. The National Council of Teachers of Mathematics recently identified problem solving as a major focus of mathematics instruction. Creative problem solving goes beyond merely finding solutions to existing problems. It is the ability to generate fresh questions and think divergently. Using the technology for creative problem solving may be the bridge between the arts and mathematics.

Problem Solving Software

Developing problem solving and divergent thinking skills is a task at which educational software excels. Sunburst Communications, for example, has many programs that promote problem solving skills. One of their programs, "The Factory: Strategies in Problem Solving," simulates a factory where three types of machines produce "products" of two dimensional shape. Students can choose from a variety of activities; the goal is to determine the sequence of machines that will produce a given figure. Children are actively involved in working backwards, analyzing the problem, creating, discovering sequences and deductive reasoning. This type of software illustrates the importance of sequencing, encourages visual skills, and the manipulation of objects in space.

Other problem solving programs give students experiences in determining patterns and generalizing from information.[2] These programs put students in situations that demand and encourage higher level thinking skills of analysis, synthesis and evaluation. A number of real world math/science problems can be tested through simulations. One example is the introductory physics program, **Laws of Motion** (EMI). There is a high level of interaction between the model (its systems and processes) and the student. Simulated experiments can be conducted in different worlds (Newtonian or Aristotelian for example). The laws of motion can be explored and compared to real world models to see which works best. **Micro-Dynamo** (Addison Wesley) is another good piece of problem

---

[2] "Robert Odyssey I." Learning Company "Bannercatch," and "Logic Builders," Scholastic, P.O. Box 7503, 2931 East McCarthy St., Jefferson, MO 65102.

solving software. This simulation deals with such issues as energy consumption or population growth in a manner that allows the students to modify various models and observes their result in the **real world.**

Learning, itself, is a form of problem solving. In our changing society, problems are seen as opportunities. Computers offer some of the best ways to develop higher thinking in an atmosphere of independent learning. Using computers, students select the problems they want to solve, arrive at divergent solutions, test alternatives and self evaluate. Whether substituting for variables and executing commands in BASIC or interacting with simulation software, children are engaged in the process of building mathematical tools. Writing original programs in BASIC or Logo, using logic (e.g., "Rocky's Boots" software, "Fun House Maze"), and interacting with problem solving software like "The Pond: Strategies in Problem Solving" and "Cactus Plot" (a program in analytic geometry) allows students to actively engage in meaningful problem solving and teaches skills within a context as opposed to fragmented learning divorced from the larger mathematics curriculum. This type of flexible and open-ended courseware provides students with a collection of new tools to study both specific curriculum skills and the broader curriculum of our culture. And it puts the **student** in control of the learning.

A major challenge facing teachers today is in preparing all students to participate knowledgeably in technology-related decisions of their everyday lives—and in the broader social context.

COMPUTERS, CREATIVITY AND BASIC SKILLS: A CONCEPTUAL INTERSECTION

Creativity is not a cliche. Nor is it a subject mined to exhaustion. Spontaneity and the creative imagination are valuable elements of achievement central to human development and freedom. Yet there is no freedom in an educational vacuum. Schools need to figure out how to encourage independent and fresh thinking in students—going beyond simply not smashing the child's natural creativity. The recent influx of computers into the schools reflects a national hope that technology can help provide fresh answers to developing thinking skills.

At the very time some are criticizing the inability of the schools to nurture children's imagination, others are pushing for renewed drill and practice in the "basics." An interesting contradiction, or not? Perhaps no more so than the distinction usually made between creativity in science and creativity in art. Both are integrally involved in our building creative existences. And both provide us with different ways of viewing reality. Likewise, computer-based learning technologies can embody powerful coherence-integrating ideas that are shared across all curricular areas. Basic skills, the creative process, and computing need each other.

Do We Have to Choose Between Creativity and Skills?

The intellectual tools developed in an area that fosters originality can be positively reflected in basic skill development. Printed letters and numbers are both abstract systems to help us understand reality. The computer brings numbers and letters into a closer proximity and helps us better understand both. Skills combine with creative factors to generate learning across a wide range of subjects. Although basic and imaginative skills may seem antithetical, one without the other can destroy itself. In reading, you need the basic subskills to even begin but without high level imaginative skill to assist in comprehension, it leads nowhere. The reverse situation is equally dismal—a great imagination aborts its potential without basic skills being in place.

No matter how creative a concept, there is an implicit connection to subskills. For either basic skills or creativity to be developed requires that each area underpin the other. It is fine to challenge the framework of narrowness that is often associated with "the basics," but dismissing skill training altogether would be a serious mistake. The trick is to get students to depart from the skills framework in a disciplined and informed fashion. Teachers, too, need to understand the basic skills that are contained within innovative elements of a child's work—and computer-based technology gives us the potential for creatively teaching the basics.

Creativity is more than originality. There is a strong connection between creativity (including originality and novelty) and basic academic skills. The notion of having to choose between the two is one of the worst mistakes we could make, for the two feed on each other.

Developing a unique clarity, style and focus is essential to any skill area. We need people who have the creative ability to raise fresh questions. At best, proficiency and performance are limited educational objectives. The goal is not simply to learn subskills—but to perfect them so that we can get at comprehension, solve existing problems, and raise new questions. The first step is to recognize that we are now in the shade as far as teaching either the basics or creativity is concerned. And we are in the dark about how to integrate computing skills into the process.

There is little question that educational computing has a role to play. In fact it has been accepted by many, including the U.S. Department of Education, as the fourth "basic skill"—after reading, writing and mathematics. (Others have identified the humanities as the fifth.) Computing would seem to be a natural for bridging the gap between the old view of "the basic" and the new concern with imaginative thinking skills.

The Computer as an Expressive Medium and Skill Builder

Using the computer for drill and "computer literacy" is what is most common in schools today. Computers **can** hold student interest on a boring task longer; what this illustrates is a danger of the technology being used to repeat the instructional mistakes of the past. Building basic skills with computer-based technology does not mean doing more of what isn't working. The technology should not be used to rerun the same old drudgery. The computer is not good or bad—it is powerful. It can be a boring workbook or electronic page-turner. It can also be the most powerful interactive learning technology ever devised.

Like words, paint or clay, the computer can also be used as an expressive medium. Skills and imagination belong together. In mathematics, for example, the act of creating requires a prerequisite skill base and some understanding of mathematical structure and pattern. Poetry also relies on the writer's mastery of language, form and meter. The computer is a medium of human expression that can be used as an extension of these skills and creativity. Imagination and the basics, poetry and mathematics can emerge from the technology together.

The rote drill approach of the educational fundamentalists and narrow thinking patterns often get "stuck" in elementary school. If we focus on subskill-rule following, this defines the kind of opportunities children will have to develop their minds. There is nothing wrong with teaching subskills but it is equally important to encourage the development of images to fill dry facts with substance. Elements of basic skills and creativity (combined with literature, mathematical patterns and art) open up a multiplicity of images which can be tapped and explored with the technology.

The flexibility of computers allows the imagination to select and combine elements on a number of levels. Mathematical patterns and drill can be readily generated—with visual models manipulated by the microcomputer for creative problem solving. Thus, the computer allows students to learn basic skills in a more dynamic manner. And it may not be too much to hope that some of what children learn on the computer will transfer to the broader context of how their skills are used in the **real world**.

Like composers who create by sitting down at the piano and making things up, the computer also allows for creative play. And this aspect of computers deserves at least equal time with basic skill building. Children using a Logo program, for example, can manipulate basic "hard" concepts in math—or create their own visual compositions with musical accompaniment. The editing process allows them to add, delete and "arrange" to their satisfaction. Computer generated visual models—whether basic skills or flights of fancy—can be manipulated with flexibility and creativity. The opportunity is created for moving across media—computer graphics, numbers, words, music, etc. Children create their own microworlds, imagine, **and** build basic skills that can be freely explored. The computer provides a language of thinking and a means of expression where permission is granted to be oneself.

Computer Models: Teaching Old Skills in New Ways and New Skills in Old Ways

Everyone agrees that encouraging creative behavior is as important as basic skills for our society. And they agree that it should be encouraged in the classroom. There is plenty of disagreement, however, over the curriculum focus and how to about fostering creative skills. The traditional notion of educators is that if fluency, flexibility and originality were systematically taught, then true creativity would follow. Unfortunately, it isn't that simple. To begin with, you had to get teachers to teach it. Secondly, fluency does't count for much if all the ideas generated are simply novel, trivial and unconnected. And flexibility doesn't help much if it clouds issues and discourages student decision-making. Even originality might be simply a social accommodation, rather than either intuitive boundary pushing or barrier breaking.

Unfortunately, most of what is taught in school (particularly in the primary grades) emphasizes rule following rather than imagination or innovation. Common school practice encourages children to be plodders who see the rules as conduits for action—rather than springboards for changing realities. Taking risks, dealing with failure, the desire to be surprised, and enjoying ambiguity are all essential elements in creative behavior. And are all difficult for teachers to model and for many students to accept. After all, simply accepting the "Imperial Mandate" from someone in authority is always easier. In the real world, we learn more about creativity from our failures, accidents, and the personal restructuring of our reality in the face of uncertainty. Taking risks in a non-judgmental environment, making mistakes, and "debugging the program" are just a few of the elements of computing that can create an atmosphere where creativity can flourish.

Certainly we need elements of fluency, novelty, originality, flexibility, intuition, and personal decision-making in building creative models. But we also need to go beyond literal understandings. The use of metaphor—using one idea to help explain another—is one avenue for making new connections in thinking and learning and giving us new perspectives. Metaphoric thinking may very well prove to be one of the most valuable approaches to teaching imaginative thinking.

Schools have always found it easier to stimulate literal thinking than place an emphasis on inventiveness. And there has been little help from researchers who seem to feel that the topic of creativity has either been mined out or view it as a minefield to be avoided. This avoidance seems strange given the fact that creativity has been formalized as a curriculum goal and included in most educational rhetoric. In spite of all the talk, there has been little serious attention to creative behavior and advances in the area have not materialized. By integrating the computer into both the traditionally "creative" and "basic" skill areas in the classroom children can learn both **and** come to understand computing.

As a dynamic communication instrument, the computer can act as a generator for creativity, skill building and uniquely productive work. Students are involved in creating new ideas and looking at old skills in a new way. Computer graphics can give visual dimension to metaphors and help students go beyond the literal in understanding what they are reading and writing about. What better way is there to insure that the basics are taught in depth than to include the basic intellectual tools and symbol systems—reinforced through exploratory manual cues, along with emphasis on student control of the learning environment helps put creative and basic skill learning within reach of **all** students. Students can be given opportunities to formulate unique solutions to problems.

Creativity and inventiveness can permeate all aspects of a child's learning. Those who say that education should do little more than teach basic skills seem to know little about those skills, less about children and nothing about learning. By using computers to manipulate basic skill models in dynamic new ways, we encourage creativity, invigorate the basic skills curriculum, and help students to find the message in the computer medium.

CHAPTER 3

MOVING BEYOND THE BASICS

THE IMPACT OF NEW COMPUTER-BASED VIDEO ON LITERACY SERVING SCIENCE, POETRY AND THE ARTS

OUR SCHOOLS are failing to help about a third of the population become literate in reading. Sixty million Americans are, for practical purposes, illiterate. This problem is growing steadily as we shift to a literacy intensive technological economy.

Schools, in cooperation with other institutions, must participate in the creation of new print and visual literacy training techniques—using the new technology and incorporating the fine arts and humanities. The tendency to concentrate on strictly technical solutions to our problems forsakes the most important aspects of technology—the human principles which underlie it. To fully participate in both technological and social developments, we must have a mental map which allows us to interpret modern hieroglyphics. Whether visual images or the printed word, literacy now requires competency in both.

In a narrow sense, technology alone can provide the means to specific job related skills. An example is America's largest and best financed educational organization, the Department of Defense. The military has developed some of our most advanced methods for helping "students" read both print and pictures. Semiliterate people employed by the military are taught to use both images and print as tools that aid in understanding. The army artillery school is just one example of an advanced educational agency using realistic video simulations, print-computer-video mixes and other progressive literacy techniques. (As we enter a new millennium, we must ask whether we want soldiering or poetry to receive the benefits of our new educational technology.)

Is it possible to mix the visual arts, humanities, video and computer controlled print technology to produce a more humanizing effect? The intellectual tools provided by the humanities (like the skills of analogue and metaphoric thinking) may very well be more useful for dealing with the technology of the future than the narrow band of linear skills being presented under the guise of computer literacy or **military science**. Already computers, like the Apple Macintosh, are making use of a broad band of visual imagery skills. And new computers will allow for a much broader range of sensory input and output—with technology going hand-in-hand with our humanness. The fact that there is a renaissance in art, music and dance at the same time as high technology becomes the dominant force in our economy is not simply coincidence. Advances in technology almost seem to force a "high touch" renaissance for the arts which in turn results in technology taking on some of our human characteristics. As high tech creeps into our lives, there seems to be a natural high touch reaction.

Technology is Changing Our View of Ourselves

Today's technology is changing the way we think about ourselves. The computer metaphor (or at least simile) is even used for describing creation—which is seen as DNA emerging from inert molecules, like intelligence "growing" from man to artificially intelligent computers. Although vastly oversimplified in the press, computational interpretations of the mind encourage us to think about the process of cognitive functioning (thinking).

Future computers will require elements from both the head and the heart. A wide range of thinking and emotional skills will be required—way beyond the narrow range of linguistic and mathematical skills we are now teaching in schools. The imaginative processing of visual, artistic, musical, movement and inter/intrapersonal skills are fusing with the technology. This technology, in turn, is not only changing the way people and nations communicate but also the way they live. The rich media mix that comes from this synthesis has the potential of adding to both our technology **and** our humanness.

Learning With Technology

Even passive video technology has proven it has the potential for helping children learn certain aspects of reading and mathematics.

"Sesame Street" and "Electric Company" really seem to work if the child hasn't already learned the skill. American telecommunications technology and programming is being aggressively exported abroad as a tool for cultural and economic relations. "The Voyage of the Mimi" is a new program that combines video, print, and computer media. This program used some of the same techniques as found in the military literacy campaigns. Computer diskettes are sent to schools along with printed booklets for the children to read—the video portion of the lesson is then broadcast.

One dimensional linear television viewing can also make positive contributions. Adults, for example, have viewed more dance and art on TV than in 100 years of ballet performances and walks through museums. Of course, the flip side of this coin is that intelligent TV viewing is often the exception rather than the rule—we can also be distracted from literature and the arts. The same television that brings us a Shakespearean play brings us ten acts of pointless violence per average hour and the visual vocabulary of the lowest common denominator. Only the most literate of the viewers can sort out the real from the unreal and the mentally expanding from the cerebrally deadening. Unfortunately, informative or intelligent viewing possibilities are usually left out of major network discussion—the emphasis being on ratings, public relations and image.

Infusing the New Technology into the Schools

The printed word will not vanish although other elements will change its character. Learning about print will continue to be a major focus in school. Just as the handwritten word did not replace speech, and the printed word did not replace handwriting—powerful electronic tools will not replace print. In fact, they may amplify **all** modes of communication. Electronic images will be added to the mix opening up possibilities that we are just starting to conceptualize.

Skills in language and the humanities will increasingly come into play. One new dimension is the digitized print structure of interactive literature—mixing print, visual images and personalized decision making. New computer programs will allow every print reader and writer to interact with the entire range of literature, language and the fine arts. But for these advances to truly illuminate our lives, we must encourage the artists and poets and philosophers among us to make their influences felt in new expressive ways.

Serving Poets and Scientists

The developing electronic technologies will have a profound effect on the four interrelated literacies—print, media, computer and the arts. We must consider all of these in what we view, teach and learn.

Computer chips are now being developed for artificial intelligence systems that allow for new forms of print, video, images and speech. AI systems will act as controlling elements in a wide range of learning devices from books to images from the world's art galleries. We will enter the 1990s with computer systems that process knowledge and images rather than simply information—allowing a vast fusion of learning styles and different media serving poetry **and** science.

Handled properly, this new technology can provide a creative and positive basis for the definition of education and foster a deeper understanding of our universe—providing both a logical and humanistic base to our national literacy efforts. All of us are, in one form or another, the guardians of the humanities in our schools. We must all be sure that the arts are articulated, rather than diminished, through the medium of computerized technology. To push the humanities aside to make room for technology will do serious harm to both.

The Future: Incorporating the Arts, Language and Technology

General print, media (the visual arts) and computer-based technological literacy will be the key ingredients for coping with both learning and science/technology problems. Music, art, and literature—as well as the ironies and ambiguities of life—are **not** mere distractions from uncovering the powerful abstractions of science and mathematics. Further educational programs will allow for a complex mixing of telecommunications, math, science, the humanities, sight, sound and print. The mix will allow us to push beyond the one dimensional sensational aspects of present-day curriculum to as much visually concrete substance as we can handle. Of course, it all depends on program producers allowing for it and viewers learning that certain forms of intelligent programming can be even more stimulating than a video National Enquirer style personification of the news. All of this will allow us to get to the meat of issues with video—rather than simply focusing on the sizzle.

Intelligent programming does not mean boredom or "talking head"—rather, it's using visual images for understanding knowledge systems by interacting with dramatic moving images. This computer-video synthesis will help us think and learn in new and exciting ways. AI chips, new hardware and software will allow for things to happen more like both real and fantasy worlds. Like a limited version of Woody Allen's "Purple Rose of Cairo," people will be able to project their images into a story and make decisions as a character while watching their visual image. And like the David Byrne (of the "Talking Heads") movie, "Stop Making Sense," the audience can get up and participate.

The possibilities for learning and literacy opened up by combining the most powerful learning technologies ever devised (television and computers) are truly remarkable. Of course it always comes back to our discipline.

COMPUTER BASED CHILDREN'S LITERATURE: AN INTERACTIVE LINK BETWEEN THE TECHNOLOGICAL AND LITERARY WORLD

Two of the more disconcerting problems facing teachers today are how to approach the new computer based learning technology (the "new literacy") and how to overcome student indifference or sheer rejection of literature and reading (the "old literacy"). Far from being opposed to one another, we now have the ability to reach toward fusion of the two—using man's richest intellectual invention, the computer, and his most powerful medium for the use of language over time, literature. With computers, we can make the affective impact of literature immediate. People hear and see things and react to them in a different manner than when print is used alone. New computer software also brings the reader into the story as an actor who can interact with the author's characters and change the whole direction of the plot.

Computers are central to the new set of tools that we, as teachers, have available to us to revitalize literature for children and young adults. What children "read"—whether in print or imagery, in a book or on a video monitor—is formative in their lives. Computers present us with the tools for enhancing and going beyond print to a new combination of interactive print and visual "literature." Technology gives us the potential for fundamental innovation in our approach to learning literacy concepts. Fresh insights can result from individuals working with computer/video/print programs.

Figure 7. Computer Composite Image.

Moving from Print to Electronic Literacy

New computer software allows children to take ownership of a story they are reading. Students change the plot, participate in the action, choose a role as a major or minor character—or simply step aside and change the direction of the action. The combination of print, computers, visual imagery and personalized action is a strong motivation for learning about all four. Motivation is one thing, effective instruction another. To be effective as an instructional tool, computer controlled literature must pay careful attention to both technology **and** instructional theory. One thing is certain, the potential is there for powerful intellectual and emotional experiences.

Interacting with literature, by entering the story, helps students have more intimate contact with the transcendental values of literary concepts. Analogue and metaphor are just two examples of intellectual tools taught through literature—both skills can be amplified through interactive computer controlled reading. Participatory stores can be an important source of knowledge for all our students—but this technique is particularly critical for the increasing percentage of our population (now clearly one third) that doesn't respond well to traditional print media. The technology could allow us to do for all of our population what has always been done for the fortunate—provide a connection to a rich literary past, present and future.

A Fresh Look at Literature

Whether using the computer or the traditional print medium (books), the goal of children's literature and the literature teacher is the same—to provide students with a variety of literary and expository material that helps them build intellectual tools and meaningful knowledge—while at the same time taking some joy from the process. The imaginative printed expression of human experience becomes enhanced when the reader takes part in it—whether that interaction is limited to the printed word or contains realistic graphics. A good computerized lesson allows the student to take ownership of the story and change the direction of the action.

Computer based technology can now tap past electronic encylopedias of literature on subjects like art, music, philosophy, history and science—opening up new ways for the student to browse and get in touch with literature on a personal basis. Creative imagination, working closely with applied technology, is starting to provide students with new avenues for reading and assimilating literary concepts. This is particularly important for that large percentage of children (about one third) who refuse to connect with the traditional printed text.

The Fusion of Powerful Technologies for Story Telling

Combining with mediums of print, television, and computers can amplify the teaching power of all three. A number of different combinations are possible. A few recently developed educational packages combine television, computer software and printed materials. Some only require an ordinary microcomputer and television set—others require a video disc player and a cheap connecting link. No technological breakthroughs are needed, just new combinations of what's already available.

Solutions Unlimited, developed by the Agency for Instructional Television, is a computer-video-book program that simply requires a microcomputer, television set and some ability to read the printed page. Children interact with a combination of electronic imagery, voice and the printed text. Such a media mix provides greater opportunities for tapping students' interests and learning styles.

Interactive video disc devices are another currently available approach to the synthesis of video, print and computers. They also have a great deal of potential for the powerful fusing of literature and technology. Using a cheap videodisc player, a microcomputer and a connecting link, children can interact with reading (both print and visual imagery) content as the laser beam jumps from segment to segment based on the student's decision making. The student uses the computer to control the actions, rather than having the computer control them. Unlike general television broadcasts, videodiscs can be almost individual in focus and specific in scope. Both NASA and the Nova programs have allowed programmers to adapt their videos and films for videodisc computer learning. A student can "tour" the moon with astronauts and do scientific experiments at the speed and direction of their interest—looking at any item of particular curiosity.[1] Programs, like those from Active Learning Systems (Minneapolis), are limited to the 50,000+ possibilities on the disc, but the student is in control of that universe. New computer formats also allow for the same kind of student control over print and pictorial information.

A single unit microcomputer/videodisc player has recently been introduced by NCR Corporation of Dayton, Ohio. NCR InteracTV is designed for educational purposes and displays videodisc images simultaneously with computer generated text and graphics, allowing the user to interact with this broad range of media. Students use a touch screen for controlling the presentation of video images, sound, text and graphics.

Rather than reading a linear print presentation of one of the world's great art galleries, videodisc devices could, for example, allow students to explore the great art and science museums of the world. They would be able to examine the details of any painting (at their own pace) and even summon up printed text to explain the picture and the artist. There are even new programs that allow for windowing (having several sources of information on the screen at once)—letting students look at pages in a

[1]Video Vision Associates Ltd., 39 East 21st Street, New York, NY, 10010 (212)777-4108.

book and related scenes from a movie version of the story. At the same time, it would be possible to summon up a print explanation of the conditions under which the writers constructed both the movie and the book. This technology also holds powerful possibilities for children to interact with all kinds of literature.

Inhabiting an Author's Environment

Another type of computer based literature requires the student to get into the middle of the action by becoming a character in the story. As a character, she follows whatever strategy she can devise, thereby moving back and forth between creating and reading. The learner defines and redefines the structure of the story in his individual style, breaking free of the linear nature of traditional print media.

Literary programs available today have a great deal of action and puzzle solving, but are far removed from joy stick controlled interactive games. They rely on the printed word to cue the player's response; however, some are starting to make use of high quality computer generated graphics. Interactive fiction such as "Zork," "Deadline," and "The Hitchhiker's Guide to the Galaxy" involve the student directly in the action.[2] The interactive story "Deadline," from Infocom Software Co., advances something like this:

Computer: You are standing at the front door of the suspect's house.
Student: (responding by typing instructions) Go around to the back door.
Computer: The back window is open. You see footprints in the soft mud where someone obviously had fled in a hurry.
Student: Follow footprints.
Computer: The footprints lead you to the suspect. "Why are you following me?" he demands.

Like the development of a play which depends on the actors' ways of handling their roles, the development of the story depends on the player's continued participation; the plot unfolds according to his response. Recreational reading software like "Deadline" and "Zork" extend a sense of realism to the reading process. Such "participa-stories" have the potential for involving students in intense intellectual and emotional experiences.

---

[2] "Zork," "Deadline," "Hitchhiker's Guide to the Galaxy," "Cornerstone" are interactive software produced by Infocom Inc., 55 Wheeler St., Cambridge, MA 02138.

Another type of participa-story is put out by Synapse Software. This interactive fiction relies less on action and more on the implications of character. For example, a panhandler might bother the student until some type of appropriate action is taken. And the story changes direction based on the student's reaction to situations in the narrative. Scholastic Software also puts out interactive fiction software which allows children to create their own stories, make decisions which change the outcomes of the tales, and participate in them via "action graphics." [3] Learning the rules of the interactive story can help students master certain rules or characteristics of literature.

Many of our schools now have interactive simulation stories that the students are reading. Just about every teacher that has turned on a computer has used "Lemonade Stand" or "Oregon Trail."[4] There is general agreement that these computer generated lessons can help increase reading comprehension. Connecting already available simulation software to related books can enhance both. Using a simulation like "Oregon Trail," for example, in conjunction with the award winning book of the same title, allows students to gain fresh insight into the printed text. Instructional simulations enable students to interact with models of other literary realities, actively making decisions and observing the effects.

Combining Learning Tools in Schools and Libraries

Libraries, which have always served as an important adjunct to schools, are now loaning out VCR tapes, computer programs, and, in a few cases, even computers. There is nothing wrong with these new possibilities for electronic interaction with literary ideas. Some of the possibilities are surprising. For example, after the teacher read several research studies that indicated that calligraphy improved handwriting, he had the fifth grade class (at our university laboratory school) use an Apple IIe computer and a $75 Koala pad to design and to print documents that looked like medieval manuscripts. Using this type of peripheral device, the children saw the similarity between drawing and writing. They also found that getting a "handwritten" letter was more personal than getting one from a word processor.

[3] "Tales of Adventure," "Tales of Discovery," Scholastic Software, 730 Broadway, New York, NY 10003.

[4] "Oregon Trail" and "Lemonade Stand" are programs put out by Minnesota Educational Computer Consortium (MECC), 3940 Lexington Avenue No., St. Paul, MN 55113.

The individually unique pages of handwritten manuscript were carefully bound and placed in the class library. In recognition of the twentieth century, a Dewey decimal number was put on the back. Since the computer could be used to print out multiple copies, students were encouraged to make notes in the margins as they read, much like the owners of medieval manuscripts. However, we also stored the program on another floppy disk so that other children could add graphics and change the structure at will. Using a speech synthesizer, realistic graphics, and an authoring system (making it possible to program in plain English), they built simulations so that others could share their work.

Human technology is changing so rapidly that we often fail to intelligently assimilate and integrate the possibilities that we create. Technological developments in computing, video, and telecommunications have the potential of dramatically transforming educational activities. But as one fourth grader in the University of Northern Colorado's lab school recently said when he received a report card that was all "Cs" and "Ds" with a handwritten note from the teacher at the bottom, saying "He has great potential," **"There is no greater burden than having great potential."**

Our Best Literary and Educational Minds Must Be Involved

Although the utility of computer based learning is with us today, it would be a mistake to judge the future role of the computer in children's literature by what is available now. In the machine, literary directions are being opened up as we constantly develop new approaches. The situation is similar to the development of printing in its initial stages. The first printed works were poor, handcrafted imitations of manuscripts. It was only later that mass productions of literary texts started rolling off the assembly lines with standard print styles. This type of book cut the time required to read the text in half. Technology changed the literary community's perception of language, reading and the acquisition of knowledge. New computer controlled electronic programs can result in equally dramatic changes.

Schools and libraries must play a role in this latest technological change or they will leave the direction of change to the teenage entertainment marketplace as parents bring such computer material directly into the home. If we abdicate our responsibilities, a promising technological art may end up like most commercial television today, taking our children's time without giving anything substantive in return. Why not take the technologies available and use them to serve our own ends, having children and young adults enter into and learn to grow with literary traditions?

Commercial decisions are being made for us with little concern for either literary or educational merit. Without involvement of our best literary and educational minds, we could lose much in the rush from print to an electronic learning medium. It would be wise to remember the fifteenth century when editors (the commerical programmers of that era), in their eagerness to get out a printed book, would buy a manuscript and set into type only those portions of a book they thought would sell. The rest was discarded and lost forever.

A Future Literary Genre?

In 1927 the Russian literary critic, Vladimir Propp, mapped out the rules governing the structure of fairy tales; in 1965 they were programmed into a mainframe computer—and in 1985 they were squeezed onto a microcomputer program. These rules can form the basis for an artificially intelligent expert system. Such expert systems absorb the knowledge from human experts, apply it in different situations, reach conclusions, and interact with the user. From literature to medicine, AI programs are getting better at emulating human thought—and they are now becoming available for microcomputers. In the near future, these artificial intelligence assisted stories will use a rule governed literary program to help students explore and create highly motivating microworlds. Even the inexpensive microcomputers found in schools today have the power to do some of this—allowing the child to play with the text, rearrange reading topics and directly influence the story. With expert systems growing more sophisticated at a rapid pace, the possibilities for various literary dialogues may move from a curiosity to something approaching a literary genre.

The educational possibilities for using this computer based literary knowledge (for human interaction, simulation, and experience) are endless. With authors like Ray Bradbury, Carthur C. Clarke, and Robert Heinlein already involved in creating software, there is a certain literary and technological momentum. It seems appropriate that science fiction writers are creating the first interactive fiction for children and many adults. Some of their interactive stories on the microcomputer software market, even in their primitive state, are engrossing numerous "readers."

Students are already using the first computer based children's literature to find new ways to eliminate evil in enchanted lands and change the characters' settings and direction in **Huck Finn**. Many children find that taking ownership of stories and situations can be more exciting and challenging than turning the page of a conventional, printed story. It also helps them build a new respect for authors of printed material—and increase reading comprehension. The technology also allows for personal interaction, based on a student's particular learning style, that goes beyond anything even imagined a few years ago. This is particularly important for those students who have rejected traditional print reading. For these children, computer interactive stories may prove to be their first (and perhaps only) link to the literary world.

Changes in How Knowledge is Disseminated

For the last several hundred years, the printed page has been the repository of our literary heritage as well as the primary means of understanding, preserving and disseminating all kinds of information and, occasionally, wisdom. Beginning in the 1960s, television began to play a large role in this same process. By the mid 1980s, various combinations of computer controlled print and visual imagery began to take their place. Just as type set print changed manuscripts in the fifteenth century, both the production and use of printed books are being changed today by computer controlled print and imagery.

Electronic literature can be collected, reorganized, molded and transmitted in order to match a student's individualized learning need. The first tools for this creative interaction of students, computers, and literature have already been fashioned. Although the printed book will continue to be important, literature can be made more accessible by use of the interactive computer program. The result can be the synthesis of print literature, computers and television. The combination is capable of accomplishing learning tasks that none would be able to do alone. The new technology can bring energy to the process of learning and help us reach the third of our population that simply doesn't respond to print. Literary concepts can permeate all of the mediums bringing intellectual depth and understanding to the enterprise.

Electronic participa-stories allow access in all kinds of unique ways. Their power to attract is as undeniably exciting as it is disturbing. As new concepts in electronic literature come into being, it is important to avoid simply moving toward the lowest common denominator, like the crassness of most of our television and video games. The future of our children's literacy (print, visual and computer) depends on what the literary community and educators do today. For teachers, the best advice might be: don't be afraid, don't be ignorant, reject the control, and enjoy being a pioneer.

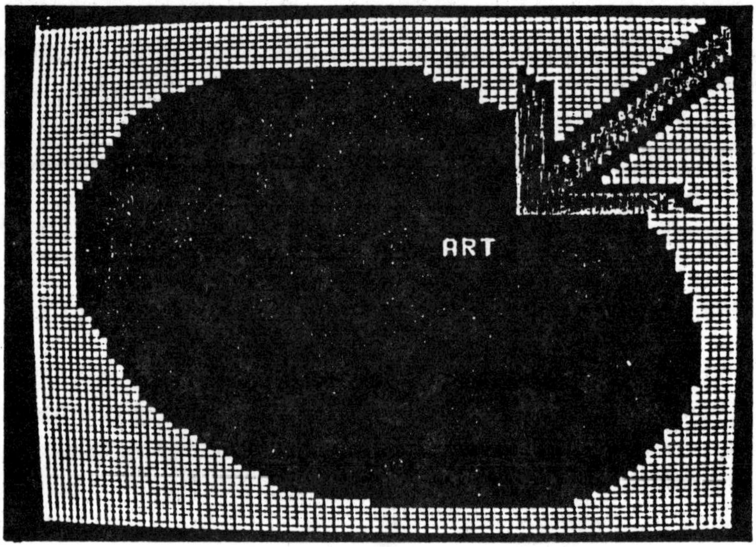

Figure 8. Computer Generated Image.

THE FUSION OF ARTISTIC AND SCIENTIFIC THINKING

At the same time science and technology are moving away from a strict focus on an empirical search for strict realities, new computers like the Apple Macintosh are appropriating an abbreviated version of the symbols, vocabulary and strategies of art. There is also a concern with precision and search for truth in the visual arts. In fact, any definition of art that doesn't include the technology its age is wrong. Unfortunately, schools often emphasize an outdated brand of both. Just as science is becoming more human and freeing itself from portraying blank certainty, we are pushing aside both the scientific method and humanistic thinking tools our students most need. Television and schools have acted jointly as great levelers of art. Increasingly, both have viewed art as a type of personal participatory therapy, rather than as a discipline worthy of its own integrity.

As the educational system focuses on a narrow range of skills, computer-controlled technology is starting to be built on a broad base of the humanities. This is happening at the very time that scientists themselves are coming to realize that art may be the most effective way to prove things about life. Life and technology really do imitate art. Science itself is making more use of the type of metaphoric thinking and perceptual skills commonly found in the visual arts and humanities. Coincidentally, we are reaching towards a new liberal arts that incorporates technology.

The human and artistic principles that underlie science and technology are more central to its utilization than concentrating on the mechanics of computers or other technological tools. These same social/historical human concerns have been slowly pulled away from art education with what little is left increasingly emphasizing hands-on production activities.

Technology is Starting to Build on the Humanities

Computers like the Apple Macintosh are beginning to make use of skills drawn from a broad band of the visual arts. Yet another type of human skill will enter computing as we, by the end of the decade, start communicating with these machines through speech. The intellectual tools required for multiple technological styles are those that must integrate many visions. New computers will allow for a wider range of sensory input and output, with technology going hand-in-hand with our humanness. The fact that there is a renaissance in art, music, and dance at the same time as high technology becomes the dominant force in our economy is not simply coincidence. Advances in technology result in a high touch cycle of reactions which in turn provides the intellectual tools for developing technology; technology is taking on more of our human characteristics.

Humans as Knowledge Processors?

Today's technology is changing the way we think about ourselves. The computer metaphor is even used for describing dreams, which are seen as "clearing the program" during sleep. Although vastly oversimplified in the press, computational interpretations of the mind encourage us to think about the process of cognitive functioning (thinking).

Future computers will require a wide range of thinking and emotional skills, going well beyond the narrow range of linguistic and mathematical skills we are now teaching. The imaginative processing of visual, artistic, musical, movement, and interpersonal skills will fuse with technology. The rich media mix that comes from this synthesis will add to both our technology **and** our humanness.

The Negative Effect of Learning Style Biases on Science and Art

Gender bias has traditionally been inseparable from the natural sciences, not just in the exclusion of women but in science itself. We are coming to recognize the consequences of subjects that have largely kept girls and women at arms length. The gender exclusion has not only affected women's roles and attitudes but also detracted from science and shaped the direction of scientific research. Though this has begun to change, schools are moving in the opposite direction by trying to reinvigorate an outmoded concept of science and technology. Calls for excellence seem to mean doing more of what's not needed. What we teach under the guise of **computer literacy** is very different from the skills needed for the present, to say nothing of the long range future.

Both boys and girls have been victimized by this unnatural gender-based compartmentalization of science and technology. The same thing has happened in art in the opposite way. Art has ceased to be seen in the schools as a serious discipline. Art is frequently viewed by educators as an effete activity and as a consequence has been pushed aside in the emphasis on competency and basic skills. It seems ironic that the skills most necessary for the future are being shuffled aside in the rush to teach the "basics." Skills gathered from the humanities provide us with the very thinking tools most needed for a technologically rich future. Not only boys and girls, but school-based art and science have themselves become victims of narrow thinking styles. This is occurring at the same time real world artists and physicists are asking the same questions.

Manipulating Art

Creative expression is a basic human need that each culture expresses through its available technology. Some cultures see the visual arts as a form of meditation that brings out the vitality and beauty of the universe. Others see it as a precious heritage—a way that reveals to ourselves (and no others) the inner vision that guides the whole enterprise. Art in all cultures uses gestures and symbols to help people take part in a universal search for meaning and expression. In America, the mass audience has made several brands of visual art (particularly video) a part of everyday life. The potential that new technology holds for producing and assisting in both visual and print literacy is partly understood. However, the relationship of computer-controlled visual images to the traditional visual arts and print literacy has yet to be explored.

Artists are using technology to explore new ways of relating to images and print. Nancy Burson, for example, has used computer controlled technology to combine the faces of five models into one "ideal" face with printed adjectives that describe the image. Besides combining the face of a woman and a cat, Ms. Burson has used a computer based image warping system to produce a single androgynous image of two nudes—one male, one female. The same artist has fed models of the aging process into the computer system—making it possible to project how a person or place might look a decade earlier or later.[5] The potential for children to add stories to these future or past images that computer controlled video can project is endless. The most ubiquitous presenter of information, the video screen, is influencing how people see even the most human of artistic images—nudes. The way we see the human image is changing, as it did in the early 19th century. As artists are trained via the video image, it changes how people are drawn and painted. Artists see the way they are trained to see and people look different on the video screen.

Just as the technology is being used to teach art, art is being used to teach technology and science—whether through three dimensional graphics, problem solving, or whatever. There are a number of inexpensive (and not so inexpensive) ways to access print, art, and science through laser video-disc-computer interface. Whole art museums can be toured in the classroom or students can interact with real astronauts on the moon. This technology allows us to amplify both art and science. Various computer controlled interfaces allow for different degrees of image interaction. Computer generated text and graphics can be overlayed onto the video-disc output. This allows print and graphics to be keyed over realistic video images of art and science. These round, interactive picture books allow students access to literally hundreds of thousands of realistic images, from a universe many of them might not ever see or

[5] This aspect of Nancy Burson's art has been commissioned by the Federal Bureau of Investigation to help find missing children. This same artistic use of technology has the potential for contributing to many areas of science.

experience. Demonstrating the tie between art and science, a computer generated image of the rings of Saturn recently won the American photography award as best art/picture of the year. Taking this computer controlled technology and matching it to the child's learning style makes learning about the outside world more efficient. To participate in that world, technology and the humanities must be linked so that sound communication takes place.

Searching for a Common Vision

A type of art and humanities instruction that nurtures creativity and deepens our understanding of the world will increasingly come into play as we move to understand our technology, ourselves, and the future. Few scientific or technical problems exist without their aesthetic, moral, economic, or social components. There are few areas of the visual arts and humanities that will not be impacted by science/technology. The combination of powerful intellectual tools are the most valuable things to be learned, whether coming from the humanities or science. Powerful art and powerful science enables us to take possession of the forms that works of art and scientific theory provide. Aesthetic methods, methods of analogue (from history), metaphor (from literature), the scientific method, and strictly technological methods will be the essential elements in future learning. We, as educators, need to include technology within the liberal arts. We need to modify how we think about scientific and technical problems, recognizing that the arts and humanities sharpen analytical and perceptual skills.

SEEING THROUGH THE MIND: LEARNING AND COGNITIVE SCIENCE

Effective learning has always been the result of methods of different instructional methods and media. Cognitive science is a new discipline that focuses on the new computer control aspect of this equation and incorporates the understanding of cognition, whether it's human or machine, real or visual. It has just begun to present us with a new way of viewing "thinking." It is changing how we conceptualize everything from teaching and learning to entertainment and information—even changing our perception of ourselves. This developing cognitive model of information processing makes heavy use of images and computer-based metaphors for explaining both human and machine learning.

The products of cognitive science provide us with a new technological lens for viewing thinking—serving to increase our understanding of how knowledge is visualized, manipulated and retrieved. The information processing model itself is derived from the ways computer scientists generally describe what machines do. Stimuli such as three dimensional data, and instructions (information) are "read in" to our knowledge network, a series of instructed manipulations are performed, information is processed, and there is some knowledge "output." This model is beginning to serve as a tool to increase our understanding not only of how to construct computers, but how to understand the human cognitive abilities and the learning process.

The relatively new discipline of cognitive science is a mixture of psychology, philosophy, artificial intelligence, computer science, education and the visual arts. This interdisciplinary mix offers fresh insights into intelligence, cognitive behavior, and multiple learning styles—providing us with powerful new tools for analyzing both human and machine intelligence. Some futurists in the field even use the analogy of the symbiosis between us and the bacteria within us and the future symbiosis between a reasoning person and computer chips.

The development of intelligent tools can amplify human intellectual capabilities in important and beneficial ways. Computer controlled, visually intensive devices are evolving into self-extensions, entering our social and psychological lives and affecting the way we think; even the way we think about ourselves. These forms of artificial intelligence build on an image rich base to assist us in our exploration of the human thinking-learning process.

Imagery Intensive Mental Models in Cognitive Science

Recent studies in artificial intelligence research suggest that the brain is able to process knowledge about objects and their functions separately from information about their shape. Our visual system enables us to recognize images without consciously naming or connecting a verbal description. This powerful process has not gone unnoticed. From the earliest prehistoric rock paintings to present day electronic graphics, imagery has served as a powerful form of communication and learning, defining relationships through pictorial, symbolic and abstract messages.

In the imagery process, objects take on realistic properties and allow us to more closely represent realistic experiences. Visual pictures occur in a mental medium which acts like a TV monitor. Images can be mentally manipulated and altered and scenes acted out. Because imagery is more concrete, closer to reality, and involves less abstract decoding, it is a powerful learning medium. The study of visual cognition is also providing us with fresh insight into our own perception process and mental functioning. One of the reasons computers have been so successful is that they allow intelligent access to three dimensional visual models—allowing us to use the video screen for exploring subjects from molecular models to classical paintings. With the helpful computer terminals, we can simulate experiences that are denied in real life. Computer controlled graphics allow students (at home or in school) to visually examine concepts that were previously explained by the printed word or in mathematical formulas. Video representations of objects can be manipulated in the mind and on the screen. This helps the user to deal with concepts more concretely—and at a greater intellectual depth—than when abstract symbols are manipulated alone.

The research supports the notion that the ability to think in images is an essential intellectual tool. And it can be taught as a collection of specific abilities—some examples here are the ability to extract meaning from pictures, understand specific symbolic details, and mentally manipulate images. Individuals can be adept at some and poor at others.

The literature on cognitive science and human mental imagery is also causing us to take a new look at individual learning styles and the impact of an electronic device that tends to deprive its audience of the level of information and analysis that it needs to evaluate the world of ideas. We spend more time watching the fleeting images of TELEVISION than doing anything other than sleeping.

Our Most Influential Medium for Vision and Symbol Manipulation

Cognitive science researchers, working on computer vision and symbol manipulation, have shed some light on human thinking in this area. For example, children and young adults have grown up with video images and have incorporated its symbolic structure into their thinking. As in computational models, this is usually done in a manner that is without ethical or political content—with empty entertainment masquerading as serious information. In many respects, television is apolitical and amoral—with imagery taking on greater significance than issues. In fact, study after study concludes that partisan bias has not been a significant factor in American news coverage. Usually there is no ethical perspective—rather a middle of the road trend toward the superficial, sensational and personal.

The essence of any cognitive system is its symbol processing ability. The medium can fluently manipulate symbols and undo the good as well as the bad. Important events and situations often get trivialized as the video medium reaches for the simplest common denominator in the picture. While the video screen is most often associated with television, its influence goes way beyond TV entertainment and news programming. These screens are now displaying print information everywhere—from the school computers to airline counters to the computer-controlled large screen at football games. The medium does indeed influence the conceptualization of the method. Artificial intelligence researchers have encountered the same problem with computer vision and manipulation. Video technology, which so adeptly manipulates symbols for both humans and machines, seems to carry with it the inherent notion that complexity is a sign of weakness. Mediocrity is further amplified when myth and the creative examination of social and political concerns (that were experienced through art) have been taken over by simplified TV images. Just one social by-product is the politics of video illusion. When we most need intelligent statecraft to survive in a dangerous world, we get images that form a powerful false reality.

The Effect of Technology on Learning Styles and Cognitive Processes

Our visual system permits us to retrieve information that is stored at a deeper level than when objects have to be retained by abstract formulas or print. To the extent that we allow the presentation of trivial images to enter our consciousness, then we are trivialized. In spite of all the negatives associated with video images, the potential is there for fusing with other technologies—allowing us to reach a broader spectrum of student learning styles. We are gradually coming to recognize that combining the powerful technologies of television, computers, and artificial intelligence can assist us in teaching students who are "intelligent" in areas that the schools neglect. Computer-based video imagery has real potential in helping reach out to musical, spatial (visual), kinesthetic (movement), and inter/intrapersonal intelligences. This newly perceived mix of multi-intelligences is intertwined with visual learning and thinking styles. As the new information technologies of television and computing begin to interact, new learning relationships start to emerge.

New teaching resources which combine print, visual imagery and computer-based technology are beginning to take form. Computer controlled pictures and sounds combine with traditional print symbols to form new connections and relationships—building on different "thinking" styles in both humans and computers.

Our knowledge of visual cognition is evolving and dramatically changing our view of ourselves and the learning processes. In learning to use both the new and old information technologies, we will be able to more fully control, label, understand and manipulate experience, and come to know ourselves better in the process. We are beginning to view the goal of education as training people to be life-long learners, to communicate and cooperate effectively with others through non-human electronic systems.

Future Visions of Both Human and Binary Learning

Cognitive science is hard at work in the study of how brains, minds, and machines are directed by levels of visual knowledge and the effect of such knowledge on learning. The new discipline will have a direct effect on all of our educational institutions as it brings together domains as diverse as artificial intelligence, the visual arts, and education. This opens up the exciting possibility of uncovering some of the mysterics of thinking—becoming a catalyst for a major re-examination of the thinking-learning process.

The computer-based technological offspring of this study of cognition can be used to engage students in a more active type of thinking and learning. And, in turn, the whole process may also be a force for encouraging the development of new models of the mind. As cognitive scientists build electronic thinking processes to help us manipulate and visualize abstract phenomenon, they must analyze cognitive functioning. The result is bound to be more powerful ways of mapping thinking and learning. The end result is bound to be more powerful teaching.

IDEAS AND ACTIVITIES

Theory and research are used to inform the practical ideas and suggestions presented here. None of the activities should be looked upon as isolated methods, but rather as general avenues of learning that teachers can personalize, adapt and incorporate to meet their curricular objectives.

Using the Newspaper to Teach Awareness

Newspaper Scavenger Hunter Activity

Use the entire newspaper. Select a day when the regular weekly science and technology section appears. Scan the paper and come up with categories which focus on computer-based technology. Make a list of the fifteen or so subject categories. Secure enough copies of that issue of the daily news so that each pair of students has one. Pass out the newspapers and a duplicated list of the categories selected. Instruct students that they have 15 minutes to search through the newspaper and circle items which fit under each category. When they locate an item, they should record the page and column number on the duplicated sheet under its category heading. At the end of the 15 minute exercise (or until the first partnership is finished) have students count up the number of items under each heading. Generate discussion. Encourage students to challenge and defend their selections. (Newspaper activities are also very useful for adult literacy classes—those "students" can begin "reading" real material on day one.)

Follow up activities:

- Have students create a story from the newspaper headlines which captured their attention or from the ideas generated in class discussion.
- Encourage students to take home the idea and discuss it with their families.
- Instruct students to look for examples on TV which support their findings.
- Create a class data base for each category or topic.

Creative Writing and Technological Literacy

Adventures in Time

Have students write a letter to a baby telling him or her about computers, technology and how the world functions today in an industrialized society. Students may wish to illustrate it using computer graphics or a Koala pad. To project ideas into the future, write a letter to a child born in 2010—what do they have to know about to get by? Then have students take an imaginative leap in time and pretend they are the baby who has grown up and is their age. The "baby" reads and responds to the letter and tells of the changes that have taken place. Some possible letter generating ideas may include students' everyday activities which involve technology, students' school experiences, hobbies and favorite TV programs.

Poetry With a Technological Theme

Working in pairs or small groups, have children go through popular magazines or technology journals to find a picture which they feel reflects technology and shows action. After they have found the picture, instruct students to do the following:

1. On line one, write a one word description of your subject or picture.
2. On line two, write down two verbs, or action words which describe it.
3. On line three, write a four word prepositional phrase or four words which say something about the picture.
4. On line four, use one word which tells what the picture is.

After this has been done individually, you can tell the students that they have created a poem. Try putting students in groups of five. Provide them with felt pens, scissors, glue and construction paper. Create a new cinquin poem about a picture the group has chosen. Cut it out, mount the picture, use large letters on the poem. Use computer, print shop program, Koala pad, and printer, if there is one available. If not, the poem can be written with felt pens and then be cut into a shape of their choice—all five placed around the mounted picture—and displayed.

Creative Writing Ideas

Creative Writing from Adventure Software

Students enjoy and often get very involved in adventure software like "Zork" and "Deadline." Turn this enthusiasm into a creative writing activity. Some story starters might be:

- How do you imagine yourself when you play the game?
- Describe the setting and favorite characters.
- Give the details of the treasure you find.
- Recount your adventure.

Letters Home

Using a word processing program, have the class work together to compose a form letter to parents. Type in the letter on the program and print out a hard copy for each student.

Processing Paragraphs

Let a word processor take the drudgery out of sequencing activities. Give students a set of mixed up sentences that have been saved on a disk in scrambled order. Explain how to move text with the word processor and put the paragraph in order. Have students create their own mixed up paragraph. This is a valuable activity for showing students how to edit using the word processor.

Group Stories

Create group stories on the computer. Assign a topic or let students generate one. The opening paragraph is started by the group. Each student must add a section to the story. At the end of the week, the story is printed out and the group collectively reads and edits the story.

Social Studies Activities

Flags for Nations

Working in groups, have students draw flags of nations on graph paper. Using BASIC programming and low resolution graphics, plot commands on the computer. Students could also use turtle graphics of Logo programming.

Traffic Signals

Create screen simulations of flashing traffic lights using the following program:

```
10 GR
20 COLOR=1
30 FOR C=1 TO 19
40 HLIN 10,30 AT C
50 NEXT C
60 FOR X=1 TO 500: NEXT X
70 GR
80 FOR X=1 TO 500: NEXT X
90 GOTO 20
```

Students can change the color command so that a green light and then a yellow light flash. From there go to making a traffic light with green, yellow and red squares. To make all three squares of color on the screen simultaneously, each square (beginning and ending values of C should be different). See if students can make their signals flash.

Historical Facts

Create a history database using a database program. Encourage students to research areas they are studying. For example, working in groups students studying American colonies could create an information database on population, settlement, industry, ports, etc. Students could then make comparisons, sort statistics, and make hypotheses based on the information accumulated.

Computer Awareness Activities

Computer Debate

Read magazines and newspapers for articles on computers (pros and cons). Clip these articles, and have students look for and clip articles as well. Present materials to the class. Each class member must decide where they stand in terms of computer issues. Form two debate teams; those in favor of the issue, and those opposed. Each team has one minute to state a case. A valid argument earns one point for the team. Those students undecided act as the judges for the debate or are assigned to one side or another.

Can You Trust a Computer?

Have students input the following information into the computer:

```
10 PRINT "WHAT'S THE TEMPERATURE?"
20 INPUT T
30 IF T 32 THEN 60
40 PRINT "IT'S BELOW FREEZING, WEAR A PARKA AND A HAT"
50 TOTO 70
60 PRINT "IT'S ABOVE FREEZING. WEAR A JACKET."
70 PRINT "HAVE A GREAT DAY!"
80 END
```

After students have run the program and experimented with several temperatures, discuss the accuracy of the computer's judgment. Encourage students to go back and change the program to make it more accurate.

Other Ideas

The Case of the Mystery Song

Some computers allow students to explore sounds and rhythms. In Atari PILOT, musical notes are represented with the command SO (sound), followed by a number from 0 to 31. SO:0 turns off the sound, PA: (pause) allows the user to control the duration of the sound. For example, PA:60 holds the sound for about a second. The following program plays the first notes of Happy Birthday:

```
 10 SO:17
 20 PA:60
 30 SO:17
 40 PA:60
 50 SO:19
 60 PA:60
 70 SO:17
 80 PA:60
 90 SO:22
100 PA:60
110 SO:21
120 PA:60
```

Students can complete this song or create a new mystery song adding rhythm or harmony. Harmony is created by playing notes simultaneously, for example SO: 1,5,8 plays three tones at once.

Random Numbers Program

Often times it is difficult to pick out a student or group of students to participate in particular activities. A random numbers program can do the job for you. Assign each student a number. Show the program to the class. (Adjust line 40 to reflect your class size.)

```
10 REM NUMBER OF THE DAY
20 HOME
30 PRINT "WHO'S LUCKY NUMBER WILL APPEAR TODAY?"
40 LET N=INT(30*RND(1)+1
50 PRINT
60 FOR R=1 TO 1000: NEXT R
70 HOME
80 PRINT
90 "TODAY'S LUCKY NUMBER IS ";N;"!"
```

Discuss random numbers with the class. Your class may wish to keep track of which numbers come up and how often. Other questions such as: "Is it truly random?" and "Why do some numbers come up more often?" are sure to arise. Some interesting activities may be to graph the lucky numbers generated or figure the percentages.

CHAPTER 4

WHERE DOES PROGRAMMING FIT INTO THE CURRICULUM?

SILICON CHIPS are those magical, miniature devices that make microcomputers work. But like a computer without a silicon chip, a computer user without a program is going nowhere. Programming, or telling the computer what to do, is a part of all computer use. Whether you choose a ready-made program disk or program directly, it is essential that the computer have a set of instructions in order to function. But just how much programming skill is needed continues to be a question of educational debate. Of one thing we can be certain—teachers and students need to have at least some knowledge of what programming **is**. Knowing something about computer languages and programming takes away some of the mystery that surrounds computers and how they work. And having a few programming skills makes it less likely that the user will assume that the program knows more than it does.

This chapter will explore the role of programming in the classroom, give a few examples (in case you want to try it yourself), and look at the most common programming languages used in education related fields. It also offers information on authoring systems, a section on expert systems, and learning activities. You are encouraged to have fun experimenting and exploring in the programming microworld of the computer.

Should Programming Be a Part of the Curriculum?

Programming courses have been taught in high schools and colleges for years. They were usually offered through the science or math department and seemed more intent on teaching students advanced calculus than about computers. It was common for the professors in some college

Figure 9. Computerchip: Emblem of the Electronic World. Computer enhanced image of a computer chip photograph.

level computer science classes to spend a month teaching physics. (In reality the only physics needed to run a computer is to understand the basic electrical principle of **on** and **off**.) Now microcomputers have brought some of the elements of Logo and BASIC programming down into the junior high and elementary schools.

With the dramatic increase in computer use throughout society, it seems worthwhile to examine the nature of programming and give some concrete examples to those who want to learn to program. In the early eighties, the initial reaction in educational computing was to emphasize computer programming. Some even went so far as to suggest that programming was essential for future citizenship and intellectual growth. It was all a little like suggesting that everyone had to be familiar with the physics and chemistry of the automobile to drive. Furthermore, unlike the foreign languages they resemble, various computer languages were shifting in importance in unpredictable ways. A great deal of time could be spent in teaching a language (like BASIC, for example) only to find that the field was moving on to another (say Pascal).

Programming isn't for everyone. For most people, the urge to learn a computer language soon passes. Some programming languages require a long period of concentrating and devotion to sequential detail. The kind of person who likes solving riddles tends to do best at it. Language skills proved more important than math skills for programming even though computer languages are not normally thought of as forms of communication. Whether a child will be good at programming and whether that individual will enjoy it are almost impossible to determine in advance. The best advice may be, **Try it, you might like it—but you may not.**

Fortunately, most computer users never need to directly program. Being able to use the computer with the aid of commercially written applications, software proves sufficient for most purposes. And although it's not as efficient as true programming, authoring systems can take your plain English and do the programming for you. A frequently voiced argument for teaching programming is the notion that we are preparing students for computer-related careers. However, the speed with which industry and business are changing is rapidly making these prevocational programming courses obsolete—particularly as new computer languages are developed and computers begin to automate by programming themselves. It is predicted that within four or five years, the advancement of computer technology and new authoring systems will cause many computer programmers (with lower level skills) to be unemployed.

While expert systems enhance the work of professionals such as physicians and geologists, they too may decrease the number of human experts that are needed. Many middle-level computer jobs (repairing both software and hardware) are being replaced by the computer. Knowledge systems now exist for many areas including: office management, medical diagnosis, manufacturing, chemical analysis, genetic engineering, and equipment failure diagnosis. Some computers have the ability to spot and repair program and mechanical problems within their own systems. As the knowledge base, problem solving ability, and human-machine interface expands, these machines may even design programs for themselves. The technology is also making it easier and easier to communicate with computers. Computer users will soon be talking to computers using normal conversational language.

Another concern regarding the teaching of programming deals with the computing teacher. It is very disconcerting for those of us who have spent many a tedious year learning the various programming languages and don't want to see our hard-earned skills become obsolete. There is the danger here of not moving with the flow of technology and becoming outdated ourselves.

The best argument for teaching programming is not to prepare students for computer-related careers, but rather to assist in the development of social and intellectual functioning. Some understanding of how programs work gives students a more realistic understanding of what programs can do and helps them function effectively in a society increasingly dependent on an information/knowledge technology. Learning logical thinking/reasoning skills of programming may also prove useful in other subject areas. For example, some of the basic logical skills acquired may transfer to reading. Other areas of transfer may include such character traits (which are required for programming) as self-discipline and teamwork.

Computer Languages

Computer languages are made up of symbols and commands which enable users to interact with the machines. Like learning a foreign language, a computer language requires study and practice. The first step for those desiring to learn a programming language is to decide which language to learn.

Computer languages basically fall into two categories: low-level and high-level. In low-level languages, the programmer addresses the computer directly in commands that it immediately understands. Often low-level languages are referred to as machine languages or assembly languages. Programs written in low level languages are usually long and tedious—thousands of 0s and 1s.

High level languages are not handled by the computer directly. They must go through the computer's central processing unit before the programmer's commands can be executed. Because high level languages are easier to understand, simpler to use and flexible among machines, they are preferred by most programmers, and most widely used. Examples of high-level languages include: Logo, BASIC, Pascal, COBAL, and FORTRAN. Each of these languages has certain properties that make it better for some applications than others.

What is the best programming language to use? There is no one answer for all users. It depends upon what you want to use the computer for. Factors to take into consideration include: the grade level of your students, your instructional goals, and your own skill and training in computer use. All computing languages have some strengths and weaknesses. Which computing language is right for you requires examining each with your specific needs and goals in mind. Remember, however, that the skill and enthusiasms of the teacher play a key part in any instructional process. So do social pressures. The closest thing we have to a consensus on teaching programming languages translates into Logo for the early and middle grades, BASIC for the middle and junior high age, and Pascal for high school students.

LOGO

Logo is an artificial intelligence language developed by Seymour Papert (and others) at MIT. Influenced by Jean Piaget, a cognitive developmentalist, Papert describes the Logo language as "a tool to think with." Children using Logo are encouraged to learn by doing and thinking about what they are doing. Logo allows young children to get the computer to do some complicated things in a way that they understand and enjoy. It helps them expand their own thinking and communicating skills while developing procedural thinking (programming skills). Young children can interact with computers without extensive training. Users manipulate visual images at a concrete level.

Papert's intent was to design environments where computers are on the same level as Tinkertoys, Lego blocks, cuisinaire rods or bicycles. Just as children design and create structures with real world objects, using Logo they are able to translate and recreate their experiences in a planned, purposeful manner. Interconnections emerge, and like the artist or poet, the child is able to clarify his own perception through the process.

When programming in Logo, the user enters the world of the **turtle**: the make-believe triangular robot who makes its home on the computer screen. Once the child enters the turtle's space, she creates her own imaginative environment using the turtle as a thinking tool.

In turtle geometry, children create drawings using familiar words like **forward, back, left,** and **right**. Powerful mathematical ideas are incorporated in children's geometric designs and cartoon drawings.

Here are some examples of how programming in Logo geometry works:

The turtle shows up as a small triangle on the computer monitor. It responds to a child's simple commands—either typed at the keyboard;

or, if the computer is equipped with a speech recognition device, the spoken word: FORWARD 60, BACK 24, RIGHT 182, LEFT 70, and so forth. FORWARD 60 moves the turtle forward 60 turtle steps, drawing a line on the screen as it moves. LEFT 90 makes the turtle rotate 90 degrees to its own left.

To draw a square with the computer, the child directs the turtle to turn 90 degrees at each corner, making all sides the same length. The student may also direct the computer to remember how to square. This can be done by typing the square directions while in the program mode, and then giving the program a name. The command TO followed by any name puts the computer in the program mode in most versions of Logo. With the Krell version of Logo for the Apple II, you can type the following directions using square as the name for the program:

```
TO SQUARE
FORWARD 100
RIGHT 90
FORWARD 100
RIGHT 90
FORWARD 100
RIGHT 90
FORWARD 100
RIGHT 90
END
```

Or some children may choose to take this shortcut:

```
TO SQUARE
REPEAT 4 (FORWARD 100 RIGHT 90)
END
```

Now, when the child types the command SQUARE, the computer carries out the new command. In this case, the computer draws a square. SQUARE is now a word in the student's own computer language and it is a command the computer understands. Programs or procedures can be called by any name the inventor chooses. SQUARE could have been called BOX, FRED, or CAT, and the computer would still **understand** it. SQUARE can now be used with other commands to draw other, more elaborate designs. Logo pogramming is designed to be done in small bits, or **mind size bytes**. Students create small programs or subprocedures, (like SQUARE), which can be put together to make a larger program. For example:

```
TO WINDOW
FD 20
RT 90
FD 20
RT 90
FD 20
RT 90
FD 20
RT 90
```

WINDOW may now become one of several subprocedures to be added to the program HOUSE.

Young children can usually program in Logo the first time they use a computer. It can also be used by skilled adult programmers in areas ranging from adventure games to scientific applications.

Being able to **"boss the computer around"** (rather than vice versa) is a crucial concept in the field of educational computing. Putting children in control of computers rather than being taught by them is perhaps the most important feature of Logo. Programming in Logo can be an empowering experience that enables children to learn and create all kinds of new microworlds. There are no **good** or **bad, successful** or **unsuccessful** thinking capabilities. Rather, different people can interact with the learning environment in different ways and learn either the same thing in different ways or different things in similar ways. This discovery-based, visible, manipulable language involves children in thinking excursions where they are encouraged to create and to make mistakes. The teacher's role is one of supporting the discovery process.

The use of Logo encourages children to collaborate among themselves, share ideas, and develop team working skills. Logo also dispels the notion of there being a right or wrong answer to a problem. The program is the problem to be solved. When a procedure goes wrong, the idea of the **bug** is introduced. Children are encouraged not to see this as a failure, but as part of the problem. Bugs are easily identified and the student sets out to **debug** her program. Many times the **bugs** lead to new discoveries and interesting results which are investigated further.

There are a number of different Logos on the market. With some, it is possible to manipulate numbers, lists of words, sprites (program modules which carry colored shapes around the screen) and tiles (static sprites). An easier version of the turtle, called **Bigtrack**, is a useful introduction to Logo.

Logo has many applications from making films to composing melodies to writing mathematics programs. The Logo programming language was developed by the artificial intelligence (AI) community. Whatever becomes of the language itself, the philosophy behind it may well carry us into the next century.

Figure 10. Computer Composite Image.

BASIC

BASIC, or **B**eginners **A**ll **P**urpose **S**ymbolic **I**nstruction **C**ode, was originally designed as an instructional language for beginning programmers. The syntax of the language is easily learned and characters and numbers can be manipulated in a straightforward manner. Despite claims of BASIC dying out, it is still a popular language due to its availability (it comes with the package on virtually every microcomputer), low cost, and the wide variety of textbooks and teaching aids that use it.

There are many dialects of BASIC, and slight variations exist from computer to computer. Programming in BASIC allows you to do all kinds of tasks: print, move graphics, provide sound—just about anything a microcomputer can do. As with other languages, BASIC involves inputting and outputting, sequencing, deciding if something is true or false, and doing something until conditions are met.

BASIC statements are usually verbs (like INPUT and PRINT) that make sense to both the programmer and the computer. These statements are always set into program lines that are numbered. The line numbers serve as labels which can be identified separately and also indicate the order in which the computer should carry out the commands. Lines are usually numbered 10, 20, 30, 40—numbers such as 11, 12, 13, and so on, are reserved so that you can later insert additional statements that occur to you. A statement is like a sentence, composed of words, numbers, and symbols arranged according to certain rules. Just as key words make up statements, statements make up programs.

BASIC Commands

BASIC commands tell the computer what to do and are acted upon immediately by the computer. They give specific information about the program to the computer system. BASIC is made up of about twenty commands that tell the computer to perform various functions.

NEW, for example, tells the computer to prepare for a new program by erasing old program statements that are in the computer's memory.

SAVE (and a file-name) directs the computer to save the program you have created in the computer's memory. If you are using a disk drive, the program is saved (stored) on the disk.

LIST will display a listing on the screen of the statements that make up the program. List commands may also be more specific. For example, LIST 50, when typed into the computer will display only line 50 (or statement 50) of the program. If you type LIST 50,80—the computer will show lines 50, 80, and all the lines of your program that fall between lincs 50 and 80.

RUN directs the computer to execute or run the program. The BASIC statements programmed will run in numerical sequence.

Variables

Most BASIC programs include variables; values that may vary as the program is RUN. Variables can be students' ID numbers, grades, names, responses to test items, etc. A variable is named or represented by any letter of the alphabet, or any letter and number up to 9. Examples of variables include: R, D5, X, Q7, etc. (The Apple II computer will allow variables to have longer names that are more descriptive of what they represent.)

There are two kinds of variables: numeric and string. Only numbers can be assigned to numeric variables. B can be set to equal 5, for example but B cannot equal Dave or Sue. The computer deals with numeric variables by treating them as values. If you assign the value 5 to the variable B, the computer treats B as having the arithmetic value of 5. Now B can be added to 2 to equal 7, or divided into 50 to equal 10.

String variables are treated by the computer as "literals." They cannot equal values. A $ is added to the name of a string variable. Nearly any character on the keyboard can be assigned to a string variable, including letters, numbers, and punctuation marks. For example, you may set the variable B$ to equal a student's name, or a student's ID number. However, the ID number would not be treated as a value, but rather as an alpha-numeric character. If you told the computer to add B$ to 2, you would get an error message. The computer is telling you that it can't add characters and values. It would be the same as telling the computer to add the word Ann to the number 2. It can't be done.

It is easy to see the differences between these two kinds of variables if you are in front of a computer. Try this:

Note that in Apple BASIC, as in most versions, any character that is assigned to a string variable must be inside quotation marks.

```
10 LET B=5
20 LET B$="5"
30 LET C$="ANN"
40 PRINT B+2
```

```
50 PRINT B$
60 PRINT C$
```

When you run this program, you should see 7,5,ANN displayed on the screen. Now add one more program line.

```
70 PRINT B=B$+2
```

When you run the program with line 70, you get an error message. On the Apple II computer, the message says "TYPE MISMATCH ERROR IN 70." In this little program, B is treated as the value 5, whereas $B is treated as the alphanumeric character and cannot be used in any arithmetic functions.

BASIC Statements

Statements are added to key words. Key words are words like INPUT, PRINT, LET, etc. All of these statements combined make a program. Think of a statement like a sentence. The program is like a paragraph. A key word such as INPUT lets you enter (or put in) numeric and/or string data. The information is entered through the keyboard and assigned to a specific variable by the program author. The variable will keep its assigned value until changed by another INPUT or LET statement for that variable.

Examples: INPUT N (for numeric data)
INPUT N$ (for string information)

A PRINT command causes the information to be displayed on the computer monitor when the program is run. This information may be either numbers of text enclosed in quotation marks in the PRINT statement.

For example: 10 PRINT "HELLO. WHAT'S YOUR FIRST NAME?"

Result on the monitor when the program is run:

HELLO. WHAT'S YOUR FIRST NAME?

LET is optional in most BASIC programs. It can be used to assign data to variables. The key word LET, followed by additional information, is an assignment statement. The expression may be a variable, a constant, or an arithmetic formula.

Example:
```
10 LET NAME$=LINDA DAY
20 LET MIDTERM=100
30 FINAL=96
```

```
40 PRINT "STUDENT," "MIDTERM EXAM," "FINAL"
50 PRINT NAME$, MIDTERM, FINAL
60 END
```

Results of Program Execution:

STUDENT	MIDTERM EXAM	FINAL EXAM
LINDA DAY	100	96

Notice in line 30, that the LET command was omitted. The program will run with or without it. Other commands include:

FOR-NEXT:	These commands make a computer perform an action a specific number of times.
REM (for remark):	Statements are used to remind the programmer of what is going on. The computer skips over REM statements when executing the program.
LOAD:	The saved program is loaded into memory.
HOME:	Clears the screen and returns the cursor to the top left.
GOTO:	Directs the computer to skip to a certain line in a program. It can also be used to make loops.
TEXT:	Reserves the screen for letters and numbers.
GR:	Reserves the screen for graphics.
COLOR:	The numbers 0-15 specify color for graphics.
PLOT:	Creates graphics, the command uses coordinates to describe the location on the screen.
HLIN:	Lights horizontal lines on the screen.
VLIN:	Lights vertical lines on the screen.

Despite its relatively simple structure, BASIC can be used to create powerful programs.

Here's an interesting BASIC program to try with students.

Hi Tech Gift Wrap

```
100 PRINT "COMPUTERIZED GIFT WRAP"
110 PRINT "TYPE IN A MESSAGE"
120 INPUT A$
130 PRINT "NOW MAKE UP YOUR OWN SHORT DESIGN"
140 PRINT "USE THE SYMBOLS ON THE KEYBOARD"
150 INPUT B$
```

```
160 PR#1
170 FOR X=1 TO 200
180 PRINT A$+" "+B$+" ";
190 NEXT X
200 PR#0
210 END
```

PASCAL

Pascal is a general purpose programming language, named after Blaise Pascal, a seventeenth century French mathematician whose work was influential in computer technology. Like BASIC, Pascal was developed as a teaching language. Its rich syntax and simple structure make it a popular language in many universities and undergraduate programs. Pascal is especially suited for structured programming and contains different sections for dividing a program into segments making it easier to understand, use and debug. Pascal combines the simplicity of BASIC with the greater capabilities of COBOL. It is a valuable language for the beginning adult programmer and provides an excellent framework for learning more complex languages.

Some of the drawbacks to Pascal are cost, and the fact that it takes more time to learn than a language like BASIC or Logo. Some college entrance tests have chosen Pascal as the computer language to be tested. However, textbooks are generally written at the college level.

COBOL

COBOL, **C**ommon **B**usiness **O**riented **L**anguage, was developed for use in industry. It is easy to use and understand and particulary adapted for writing files—a major application in commercial settings.

Instructions in COBOL are less concise than other languages and COBOL does not lend itself to structured programming. The COBOL language requires a large amount of main computer storage and is used mainly in mainframe applications.

Many vocational/technical high schools are beginning to offer training in COBOL for their students. Its procedural syntax is easy to learn and although there is a large amount of typing involved in setting up a program, it is designed for the beginner.

AUTHORING PACKAGES

Authoring languages and systems allow teachers to program in an easier manner than would be possible using a computer language such as BASIC or Pascal. Authoring packages fall into two categories: authoring systems, and authoring languages.

Authoring systems are software programs that require no programming skill whatsoever. A series of prompts allow the user to insert the kinds of information and questions desired. A number of possible correct and incorrect answers can be added to the program by the teacher—in plain English—allowing students using the computer to receive immediate feedback and evaluation on their responses.

Authoring systems enable teachers to plan lessons from an instructional point of view following a predesignated framework. Older authoring systems were criticized as being simplistic **toy** languages. Others have been criticized as too restrictive; with many of their drill and practice modes being based on principles of linear programmed instruction.

Fortunately, most of the new authoring programs are capable of producing a broad range of adaptive, interactive instruction. Students may be branched to alternative lessons or practice based on their choice and mode (sound, graphics, print, animation) of selection, diagnosis, level of difficulty or other types of accommodations. Adaptation to meet individual differences may be under the student's own control or that of the program. Good authoring systems are adaptive and interactive, with a high level of learner involvement. As with anything else in computing, we must pay attention to the characteristics of effective instruction in designing authoring systems for school use.

New authoring systems are flexible allowing many types of adaptations such as test construction, interactive testing, recordkeeping, and the creation of original instructional materials. Most are designed to interface with other systems. Examples of authoring systems include BLOCKS, CAIWare, EDUGRAMMAR, GENIS, MICRO-INSTRUCTOR, and PASS.

New authoring languages give the inexperienced user more flexibility. This allows a teacher to create the framework of the program—rather than being bound by the existing framework as with the older authoring systems. Users create statements similar to those of BASIC or Pascal. Authoring languages like **Super Pilot**[1] are organized in an

[1] Apple Super Pilot. Washington Computer Services, 3028 Silvern Lane, Bellingham, WA 98226.

instructionally meaningful manner. **Super Pilot** consists of mnemonic key commands with a simple syntax. The expansive language is simple to learn and use. Some commands include:

t: type text onto the screen
a: accept student's input to the program
m: match student's response against a predicted response
j: jump to another part of the program
u: (use) instruction can pass control to a subroutine
e: end a subroutine or a lesson
g: can produce turtle graphics
s: creates a wide range of sounds
k: keep, used for record keeping

Authoring languages can be used alone or with interactive video (the merging of microcomputer and videodisc instructional technology). Simple authoring commands can be used to control the presentation of video, text, and graphics.

Once the operation of any authoring language or system is learned, however, there is still a lot to creating a good computerized lesson. Programs may revert to a series of questions and answers if the user knows little about good instructional design or effective integration of sound and graphics. Creating any piece of instructional software requires time, imagination, and determination. Some programming skill is also required if using an authoring language. A good piece of software is like a good lesson of any kind. It requires planning, imagination and effective execution. Many courses are available today to assist educators in creating software for classroom use. Using journals like **Byte** and **Classroom Computer Learning**, teachers and upper grade students can get programming ideas. The programming is already in print. Children can copy and adapt programs to fit their needs.

EXPERT SYSTEMS

Educational expert systems are an artificial intelligence approach to learning which make computer-based education more powerful and easier to use. The development of these instructional systems enables the computer to model the **best known** means of teaching a particular performance skill. The systems communicate with the user in a natural interactive way much like an **expert teacher** teaching the subject they are best able to teach. These expert systems consist of a set of rules and a database of knowledge to which these rules can be applied. A number of tools are available which makes it easier to create new systems. Some of these include: ESP ADVISOR, Expert Ease, INSIGHT, and PERSONAL CONSULTANT.

COMPUTER BASED EXPERT SYSTEMS THAT AID ADMINISTRATORS IN DECISION MAKING

Applied artificial intelligence is just starting to play a role in management and administration. We are watching the debut of decision support microcomputer software that can improve organizational and personal administrative skills—from negotiation—to motivation—to strategic financial planning. These programs are based on knowledge, "tricks of the trade," inference, exceptions to the rules, and reasoning from a knowledge base. Some programs even allow knowledge to be constantly updated—without changing the program. In constructing an expert system for management, the computer "knowledge engineer" must interact with one or more human experts in the area to be developed or simulated. As the expert observes the operation of the system, the program is refined by adding more guidelines, rules and a restructured knowledge base.

New microcomputer management systems can help administrators be more productive. Programs, such as "Leading Effectively," provide help in moving from management intentions in a particular situation to strategies and the probability of certain results.[2] These programs provide some of the same information to higher level administrators as was previously provided by middle level managers. They can also help these middle managers move up before they are partially replaced. Using this leadership software allows you to evaluate your own leadership style and compare it to both the opinion of subordinates and national norms. Whatever the combination of formal authority and subtle influence, managers are given the opportunity to assess their administrative behavior and evaluate the results of changes. Valuable concepts about leadership style can also be learned as decisions are made in a number of simulated or real leadership situations.

---

[2] "Leading Effectively." Thoughtware Inc., 2699 South Bayshire Drive, Coconut Grove, Florida 33133.

Features of Knowledge Processing

Knowledge based systems are large data bases of information with a collection of rules (supplied by human experts) that can be applied to that data to produce solutions to problems. These systems collect and code data in a manner resembling specialized human expertise—with magnified memory capacities. Facts are compared and inferences are made based on accumulated (digitized) knowledge of past situations. Expert systems rely on a knowledge base rather than numbers; an electronic imitation of human thought processing. Unlike procedural programs which execute instructions in a predetermined sequence, knowledge based systems use sets of unordered rules which are evaluated to report the best match between information. Decisions are suggested and simulated problems solved based on inferential "reasoning." Knowledge processing systems "know" more about the real world than the narrow confines of a single problem solving environment. They are able to deal with uncertain judgmental concerns and suggest solutions along with the percentage of "certainty" or "risk."

Usually, expert systems have a natural language interface (English, French or Japanese for example—as opposed to FORTRAN or BASIC) which allows the user to interact with the knowledge base easily. New "front end" natural language systems such as "Intellect" developed by the Artificial Intelligence Corporation (Waltham, MA) allow administrators to use their natural language for developing knowledge processing systems. There is no need to rely on systems analysts, programmers or a centralized computing center. By the 1990s, we will be speaking directly to computers, with keyboards being as peripheral to the process as speech synthesizers are today.

Constructing a Knowledge Processing System

Once a knowledge base is constructed, containing whatever information is needed for the applications, a standard text editor program can then be used to compile the facts and rules. All of this is programmed in plain English. Administrative support structures can be built without any specialized computer background. The software developer supplies the ready made program. Thoughtware Inc. or Human Edge Software are two good examples of firms supplying decision support systems, with an average cost between $50 and $500. The administrative knowledge system is ready for consultation after the information is loaded onto the reasoning program. The program will ask questions, the user responds, and the computer makes inferences and suggests possibilities.[3] Most programs will not actually make the decisions—rather they force the user to organize and express the reasons behind decisions—and suggest future possibilities given certain choices.[4]

It is important to be able to ask the program how and why it reached its conclusions if the user is to fully evaluate the suggestions and get at the inferences behind projected solutions. Although the first of these microcomputer decision support systems is just starting to be implemented, the most recent do allow the user to ask for an explanation of the reasoning process.

An expert system can focus on almost any aspect of management. For example. Thoughtware, Inc. has a microcomputer program for Apples and IBM PCs called "Managing Time Effectively" that focuses on how the administrator uses time. It recognizes time wasters and organizational guidelines. Similar programs from the same company focus on leadership assessment, motivation, conducting meetings, performance evaluations, interactions and goal setting. Such elements can create an action plan for managers at any level.[5]

Computer Decision Support Systems and Administrators Are Natural Partners

Decision support microcomputer software is a set of administrative tools that just about any one can use to solve management problems. The programs themselves are among the first practical application programs drawn from artificial intelligence research. This software is aimed at solving qualitative, rather than simply quantitative, problems. It's a tool that can help administrators manage their decisions and bring more organization to decision making. The influence of such programs will grow in all areas of management as knowledge maps of various management areas are digitized.

[3] In the U.S., major corporations with large commitments to this type of research and development include: International Business Machines Corporation, Armonk, NY; AT&T Bell Laboratories, Murray Hill, NJ; Xerox Corp., Palo Alto, CA; Digital Equipment, Maynard, MA; and Hewlett-Packard Co., Palo Alto, CA.

[4] An example here is "Lightyear" by Lightyear, Inc., Santa Clara, CA. The system can classify data, select matches and evaluate potential decisions—allowing the user to supply the conclusion.

[5] Thoughtware, Inc., 2699 S. Bayshore Drive, Coconut Grove, FL 33133, (305)854-2318.

General expert systems take implicit knowledge and make it explicit—allowing the user to obtain, analyze, play with "what ifs" and model information without intermediaries. As far as computer based expert systems are concerned, the executive must think through the discrete elements of the particular decision making problem. Once this is done, administrators are able to get advice on many situations and amplify their leadership thought processes. Of course, one of the biggest problems for the designers of decision support systems is quantifying the dark corners of the administrative thinking process. Surprising, this is **not** an impossible task—and once specific management areas have been captured by an expert system, microcomputer programs will become a tool in administrative decision making. The edge they give is not inconsequential. And we can anticipate computer based management systems exploding on the scene in the next five years—let's hope that we can control the direction of the blast.

Using the New Technology to "Bother" Subordinates

In psychological studies of administrative motivation, it was found that executives described their jobs in terms of power, judgment and inter/intrapersonal skills. A surprising number, however, seem to take pleasure in simply being able to bother others. And there's a computer program that fits right in. It sends out nasty memos guaranteed to bother the receiver.[6] There is a similar program that can go beyond simply bothering to firing. Managers can practice "sacking" techniques with alternate scenarios before dismissing an employee. Other programs monitor every aspect of human professional behavior to be sure that employees "fit in." Are these administrative behaviors the ones we want to encourage? Is it possible that we will simply end up amplifying administrative mediocrity?

Tree-Structured Electronic Managers Improve Decisions

The manager can place a short or long term goal at the top of the pyramid (or tree). The user passes through six levels of decisions to reach the desired objective. Resources are limited and the administrator must balance competing concerns. The program forces users to prioritize both objectives **and** alternatives.[7] A related approach provides

---

[6] Lightyear, Inc., Santa Clara, CA.

[7] "Expert Choice." Decision Support Software Inc., McLean, VA. This program offers a relatively powerful method for developing expert systems on microcomputers.

a method of brainstorming ideas, outlining projects, and placing documents (which can be graphs, numbers or words) within a strategic outline.[8]

Building Toward the Future: Realistic Computer-Based Models of Administrative Judgment and Choice

We are in an age when crucial decisions must be made quickly, efficiently and accurately with as much professional expertise as possible. Interactive microcomputer programs available today can speed up the process and give the decision maker expert (interactive) advice on alternative administrative selections. These programs also allow managers to quickly explore various situations that might stem from decisions. This makes it possible to analyze the effect a change in one aspect of that model might have on the whole.[9] As a result of their suggestive power, they are starting to take their place as a valuable management tool for a structure and theoretical understanding of the decision making process.

These programs are, in many ways, the most intellectually sophisticated software yet developed for the microcomputer. And they are the most likely development yet for bringing executives directly into the computer using process.

Is There a Future for Administrators?

In the future, we will have programs that can perform more humanlike functions and further extend decision making and administrative skills. Already a few middle management positions have been digitized. We are rapidly approaching the day when every higher level administrator will have a portable electronic advisor containing the knowledge of top experts on administrative topics from budgets to negotiation to strategic planning. Still, no matter how advanced decision support systems and artificial intelligence programs become, the final word, for at least the next decade, will come from the administrator who uses such systems. Executive decisions may become more informal, organized and flexible—but in the final analysis, these computer systems are not ready to replace human judgment.

---

[8] "Framework." Ashton, Tate.

[9] "Expert Choice." Decision Support Software, Inc., McLean, VA.

By the beginning of the next decade, advanced versions of decision support software will be able to carry on verbal discussions with managers. Artificial intelligence experts also predict that programs will soon be capable of demonstrating a wider range of administrative reasoning power—software that more fully represents duplication of the human cognitive process. Not only will inference, association and learning be part of the process, but also speech, text, graphics, sensory perception and, yes, eventually intuition. With these developments, we can anticipate increasing acceptance and reliance on decision support programs in nearly all areas of the management process. Still, human administrators will be necessary for the forseeable future—in spite of the fact that artificial intelligence "knowledge engineers" have the long term goal of developing computer systems that surpass human capabilities in administrative strategies, reasoning, problem solving, sensory analysis and environmental manipulation.

Resources

"Artificial Intelligence—MRS" for DEC-20 with MacLisp, Symbolics, Inc., Lisp machines with ZetaLisp, and VAX with UNIX and FranzLisp. This is a knowledge-based and problem solving system designed to aid in building expert systems; $200 to non-profit institutions. Stanford University, Heuristic Programming Project, Department of Computer Science, Stanford, CA 94305.

"Artificial Intelligence Age-1," for PDP-10 and DECSystem-20 using TENEX or TOPS-20 operating systems; VAX using VMS or UNIX operating system; and XEROX 1100 Series InterLisp=D work stations. A software library for building knowledge-based application programs; $500. Contact Thomas C. Rindfleisch, Stanford University Heuristic Programming Project, Department of Computer Science, Stanford, CA 94305; (415)497-9373.

"Artificial Intelligence EMYCIN" for DECSystem-20 using TOPS-20 operating system and VAX using VMS or UNIX operating system. Helps experts develop rule-based consultation programs, supplying facilities for encoding knowledge of the domain into production rules; $200 for non-profit organizations. Contact Prof. Bruce G. Buchanan, Department of Computer Science, Stanford University, Stanford, CA 94305; (415)497-0935.

OZ: Management Control. Fox & Geller, Inc., 604 Market Street, Elmwood Park, NJ 07407.

DSS Optionware. DSS Development, Corporate Place, 4 Barnard Lane, Bloomfield, CT 06002.

Writing is Thinking. Kapstrom, Inc., 5952 Royal Lane, Dallas, TX 75230.

Lightyear Inc., Santa Clara, CA.

Thoughtyear Series. Thoughtware, 2699 South Bayshore Drive, Coconut Grove, FL 33133.

The Human Edge. Human Edge Software Corporation, 2445 Faber Place, Palo Alto, CA 94303.
Expert Choice. Decision Support Software Inc., McLean, VA.
Framework. Ashton-Tate, Culver City, CA 90230.
Teknowledge Inc. 525 University Avenue, Palo Alto, CA 94301-1982.
Expert Ease. Jeffrey Parrone and Assoc., Inc., 3685 17th Avenue, San Francisco, CA 94114.
Expert-2. Miller Microcomputer Services, 61 Lake Shore Road, Natick, MA 01760.

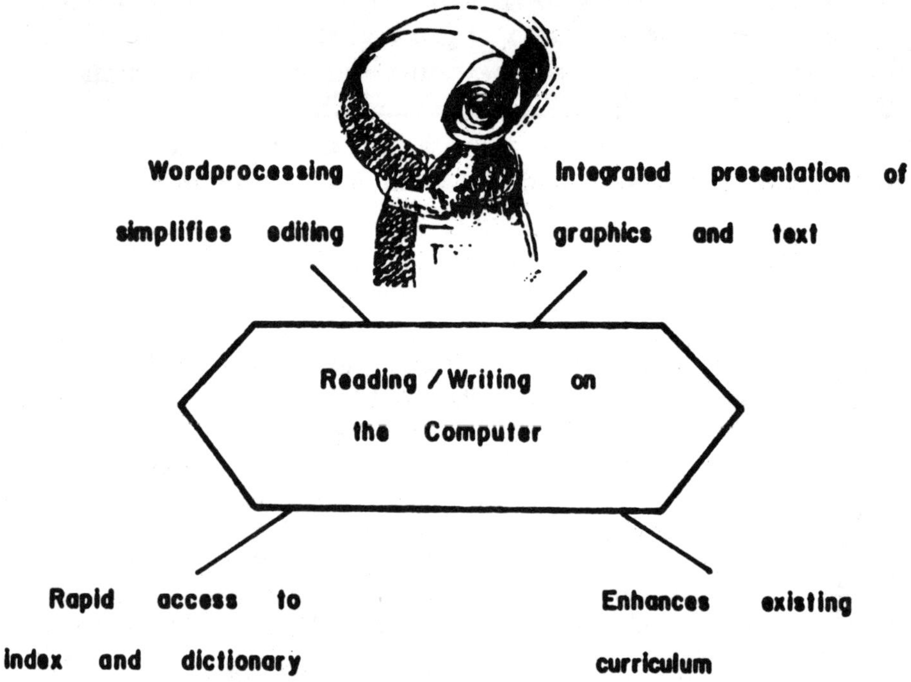

Figure 11. Computer generated images of reading and writing on the computer.

PROGRAMMING ACTIVITIES THAT CAN BE DONE ON SCHOOL MICROCOMPUTERS

Children enjoy games. And game programs do not have to be long and complicated. Here are several BASIC programs that demonstrate some important BASIC concepts and are fun to play. Children can try these with no prior programming knowledge. Variations in BASIC exist from computer to computer. Please check your manual before beginning.

Program 1 - Crazy Sentences

This short program is only 13 lines long and user friendly.

```
 10 HOME
 20 PRINT "YOU CAN MAKE A CRAZY SENTENCE."
 30 PRINT "THINK OF SOMETHING THAT MOVES."
 40 PRINT "TYPE YOUR ANSWER AND PRESS RETURN."
 50 INPUT M1$
 60 HOME
 70 PRINT "NOW THINK OF SOMETHING YOU CAN EAT."
 80 PRINT "TYPE YOUR ANSWER AND PRESS RETURN."
 90 INPUT M2$
100 PRINT "NOW PRESS ANY KEY."
110 GET A$: IF A$=" " THEN 110
120 HOME
130 PRINT "THE"; M1$ "KISSED THE"; M2$; "."
```

Program 2 - Spell that Word

Two students or two teams can play this game. One student or team enters a spelling word while the other is not looking. The word will be displayed on the screen for a brief second then disappears. The computer displays a ? prompt. The designated player then spells a word by typing it and pressing return. If the spelling is correct, the computer prints "YOU'RE CORRECT!!" If it is incorrect, the message "YOU'RE WRONG—IT'S ______" shows up (______ being the correct spelling).

```
 10 HOME
 20 PRINT "TYPE IN A WORD"
 30 INPUT M$
 40 HOME
 50 PRINT "TYPE ANY KEY WHEN THE PLAYER IS READY"
 60 GET A$: IF A$=" " THEN 70
 70 HOME
 80 PRINT M$
 90 FOR P=1 to 500:NEXT P
100 HOME
110 INPUT A$
120 IF A$=M$ THEN PRINT "YOU'RE CORRECT!!"
130 IF A$≠ M$ THEN PRINT "YOU'RE WRONG—IT'S";M$
```

Program 3 — Name That Word

This is a more sophisticated program. It can be played with two students or two teams. One player or team looks away while the other enters a word (long words work best). The word disappears and the computer asks the player to type any key to start the game. The first time through the loop only one letter of the word is shown. The player tries to guess the word based on the clues given. If the player guesses the word correctly, points are awarded for his team. Points are determined by the remaining number of letters in the word. If the guess is incorrect, the computer indicates an incorrect response was given and tells the number of points remaining. The next team member gets to view two letters of the word and take a guess. The game continues. When a word is guessed correctly, roles reverse and the opposite team can now take its turn at **naming that word**.

```
10 HOME
20 PRINT "THINK OF A LONG WORD."
30 PRINT "TYPE THE WORD AND PRESS RETURN."
40 INPUT M$
50 L=LEN(M$)
60 HOME: PRINT "GET A TEAM TO GUESS THE WORD."
70 PRINT: PRINT "I'LL SHOW YOU ONE LETTER OF THE WORD AT A"
80 PRINT "TIME. EACH TIME YOU GUESS WRONG, YOU"
90 PRINT "LOSE ONE POINT. THEN I'LL SHOW YOU ONE"
100 PRINT "MORE LETTER AND THE NEXT PERSON CAN TRY"
110 PRINT: PRINT"PRESS ANY KEY TO START"
120 GET A$: IF A$=" " THEN 120
130 HOME
140 FOR T=1 TO LEN(M$)
150 PRINT LEFT$(M$,T)
160 INPUT "YOUR GUESS:";G$
170 IF G$=M$ THEN 230
180 PRINT "WRONG—YOU'VE GOT";L-T;"POINTS LEFT."
190 PRINT "PRESS ANY KEY TO GUESS AGAIN."
200 GET A$: IF A$=" " THEN 200
210 HOME
220 NEXT T
230 PRINT "YOU'RE CORRECT!!—YOUR SCORE IS";L=T
```

In real life there are many times when a programmer must work backwards to come up with a finished product. This program offers students a challenge of working backwards to produce the result. It is suggested that students work in pairs on the project.

Program 4 - Working Backwards

Can you create a program whose output looks like this?

```
WHAT IS YOUR NAME?
? ANN
NAME AN ANIMAL
? DOG
NAME AN OBJECT THAT RHYMES WITH DOG
? LOG
NAME A PLACE THAT RHYMES WITH DOG
? GROG
TYPE A NUMBER
? 99
ANN'S RHYME
A PERSON NAMED ANN FROM GROG
ONCE OWNED 99 BREEDS OF DOG
THEY MADE SUCH A NOISE
THAT ANN CALLED THE BOYS
AND THEY PUT THEM ALL OUT ON THE LOG.
```

Some students may need additional practice before attempting to program backwards. For practice, have students try this. (Note boy, food and girl are all string variables.)

```
10 Clear the screen.
20 Ask for a name of a boy in your class. (a PRINT line).
30 Wait for the answer and give it a string variable code name.
40 Ask for the name of a girl in your class.
50 Wait for an answer and give it a code name.
60 Ask for a kind of food.
70 Wait and give it a string variable code name.
80 Clear the screen.
90 Remind yourself the story begins here.
100 PRINT (boy) BROUGHT (girl) SOME (food)
110 PRINT (boy) LOVES (food) and (girl) HATES (food)
120 PRINT (girl) THROWS (food) AT (boy)
130 PRINT NOW (boy) HATES (food) AND (girl) EATS (food)
140 PRINT CAN YOU IMAGINE THAT!!
```

Program 5 - Teaching for Next Loops

For Next Loops, tell the computer to do something a certain number of times. Children often have difficulty understanding this concept. Programs such as these may aid in the understanding and give students practice with the concept.

```
10 FOR X=1 TO 10
20 PRINT "HI"
30 NEXT X
```

Now make this program blink!

```
10 PRINT (shift) (clear home)
20 FOR A=1 TO 500:NEXT Z
30 PRINT "HI."
40 GOTO 10
```

CHAPTER 5

COMPUTERS AND STUDENTS WITH SPECIAL NEEDS

MAINSTREAMING: USING THE COMPUTER TO ADAPT CURRICULUM FOR CHILDREN WITH SPECIAL NEEDS

WE ARE JUST BEGINNING a period of expansion for both education in general and educational computing in particular. In the overall school setting, the number of microcomputers in classrooms went from about 300,000 in 1983 to nearly 2,000,000 by the end of 1986. This increase was seen at all grade and subject levels. But the percentage of increase in special education was even higher. Special educators, it seems, are less resistant to new technologies that help them reach children who do not learn in the usual ways.

The "least restrictive environment" of Public Law 94-142 means putting most children with special needs into the regular classroom for at least part of the day. Today, both the special educator and the regular classroom teacher have the responsibility of providing adaptations of the regular curriculum to meet the needs of special students. Mainstreaming and doing Individualized Educational Plans (IEPs) should not be viewed as a meaningless kind of busy work. It isn't. Rather, IEPs are an essential part of education for children with special needs. And soon they may be used with all children. There are even a number of new IEP microcomputer programs that can help ease the process. But simply supplying computers to the schools, software to teachers, and courseware to students should not be equated with meeting special needs or having a program.

Beyond Hardware and Software

Before yielding to the impulse to purchase equipment and programs, we must consider which special needs are best dealt with by microcomputers. For those applications best served by computers, we must remember that the cost is higher than the cost of the computers and software. It also involves staff development, peripherals, graphics tablets, touch sensitive screens, prosthetic devices, voice recognition programs, light pens, joysticks, large print controls, consumables, maintenance, security, modems, telephone lines, and electrical wiring. The cost of the computer itself (hardware) and a small supply of programs is just the tip of the iceberg in meeting the needs of students who do not learn in the usual ways.

Staff development is the key consideration and cost. We must have thoughtful teachers involved in determining how computers can best assist them, for they are the ones who must put any program into operation. Special educators are in as dire need as regular educators when it comes to thoughtful plans for the entry of microcomputers into their classrooms. You don't need a ten year plan set in concrete—but teachers need some training and knowledge about how things will fit into the curriculum **before** large numbers of computers arrive at the school.

Engaging the Unmotivated in Computer-Based Learning

The way computer education is currently being handled in some schools seems to be alienating special needs students—and some of the average students. Autonomy and self confidence are important elements in motivating special students. But if computer education is simply patched onto the traditional rote-work aspect of the school curriculum, then it will not be very meaningful. Students who cannot learn in the usual pattern will not be very motivated by the more efficient delivery of what doesn't interest them. Part of the problem here is that special educators have not yet developed a consensus as to how computers can be most effectively used. But of one thing we can be certain, it's a misuse of computing power when they are used for instructional tasks best performed by other media—such as flashcards or workbook pages.

Arousing awareness and developing a student's latent abilities is not easy—with or without technology. But the earlier the identification, diagnosis and placement of gifted and handicapped students, the easier it is to solve problems of poor motivation and underachievement. Digitizing the SRA cards won't do it. Rather than working on such computer-based activities as drill on the multiplication tables, students need to interact, create, and control what the computer is doing. Let's look at successful examples of using the computer for student controlled applications.

We taught students with special needs how to construct software—before they were mainstreamed into the regular classroom. Using authoring systems to by-pass programming skills, they were successful in getting an integrated team of students to develop software as a class project.

Another successful computer-based program for students who do not learn in the usual manner involved publishing a class newspaper. With the help of an Apple Macintosh computer, the newspaper looked very professional. It gave the children a sense of power over things in the real world and helped them learn basic skills in computing, writing and reading—and helped the communication between school and home. Most importantly, computer-based activities helped cut through the isolation from their classmates.

Word processing programs are very valuable communication aids for those students who have difficulty with writing. For the first time, many are able to see the fruits of their labor in a neat print format. Prompts, prewriting, composing and rewriting activities enable the student who has difficulty with penmanship, construction, and writing to achieve success.

Whether gifted or handicapped, children with special needs fall off the profile of how children learn. Some are capable of extraordinarily high performance and are bored by the usual school curriculum, while others require special services because of intellectual, physical, social, and/or emotional disability. Of course, students with special needs have the same needs as other children. The difference is that these students have less access to learning, and special teaching techniques are needed to help meet **normal** needs. This is particularly true in the area of communication skills. The computer is an ideal tool for opening learning windows and helping handicapped students communicate.

Students Do Not Automatically Like Computers

We cannot forsee the world in which our students will live. Neither can we assume that the touted **Computer Age** will be appreciated by tomorrow's leaders and citizens. If students do not understand how computers work, they may not be able to fulfill social responsibilities concerning future computer use.

Computers are not a learning resource that is the exclusive property of the more wealthy children or middle class students who are headed for college. Cutting less advantaged students off from computer-accessed knowledge is clearly seen as wrong. However, keeping the same students from the same knowledge because they lack the motivation to reach for it is more subtle and more insidious. A lack of understanding about how computers work and what they can do may contribute to special needs students losing interest in them. Contrary to public opinion, children do not automatically value computers. If special education students stay away from computers because of misconceptions about what they are, and who should use them, then they are playing at a disadvantage—both in the school mainstream and in career options.

Giving students free access to school computers during recess, lunch and after school helps familiarize them with these tools in a relaxed environment. When children and their friends use computers at home, it helps provide them with a better understanding of these electronic machines. This in turn leads to more interest in computing.

Computers can act as a stimulus in many special learning situations, both in school and at home. When the technology is used as a communications vehicle, between the home and school environment, then that alone is a major contribution to a child's learning. Understanding what computers are, how they function, and how they use information makes them an ongoing and concrete part of a person's environment. And understanding the implications, it seems, results in intelligent use.

We should not assume that students with special needs will automatically become excited when a computer is introduced into the classroom. Educationally, there may be as much of a need to motivate special education students to use computers as motivating them to use books. Once they figure out what they can do with the machines—use and learning often takes off. Microcomputers are devices that can provide the right level of mastery, success, and control for children with special needs—enabling them to approach subjects they were previously failing.

Computers are an innovation that reaches across the field of education. In terms of changing the existing educational structure, the impact is as dramatic as the printing press. Neither has (or had) a chance to replace human teachers. However, both books and computers change the **role** of the teacher—and both place a greater responsibility on them. And when mainstreaming gets added to this mix, the pressures on the professional teacher are extraordinary.

Making Sense of an Increasingly Complex and Confusing World

Special educators must do more than transmit what is and what has been—planning for a very ambiguous future is now equally important. Adapting to diversity is essential as schools change to meet future needs. The various movements for educational reform expect all students to take tougher academic courses. There is less of an emphasis on crafts and play. Even kindergarten children spend more time learning the sounds of the alphabet, beginning to print, and testing their skills on computers. When today's children (some of whom will be graduating in the 21st century) enter school they are more sophisticated (thanks to society and the media) than their predecessors. Therefore, there is a stronger focus on laying the foundation educationally as well as socially. The computer helps students with special needs emphasize what they **can**, rather than what they **can't** do. It also gives children who are easily frustrated the kind of individual attention that is impossible from one teacher.

It seems clear that computers can help special education students communicate with sound, print and pictures. With an inexpensive Apple IIe computer, programs like **Print Shop**, and a peripheral like the **Koala Pad**, these children can cooperatively design everything from class newspapers to personalized greeting cards and announcements. The computer can also help break down the barriers between children with special needs and the rest of the school population. Computers are extending the special educator's effectiveness at all levels. As these teachers become successful with educational computing, they are among its strongest proponents.

Giving special education students some special skills in computing and cooperative learning before students in the regular classroom receive that information will allow the special needs child to be seen in a more positive light (having a desired skill) when they are mainstreamed. Of course, some students must be taught the social skills needed for collaboration **and** be motivated to use them.

Mainstreaming: The Foundation of Special Needs Instruction

The concept of mainstreaming is not a movement of the moment. It has been with us for ten years now and is more than holding its own. Both the research evidence and the law agree that locking children into special social and educational environments is debilitating. Special children need to keep up with mainstream children emotionally, socially and academically. With the increased academic demands in the regular classroom, it is becoming increasingly important for special education students to get a handle on academics. The nurturing of coping skills is not a substitute for intellectual involvement and learning.

Comprehension, analytical reasoning, problem solving, analysis, knowing something about this country and the world, a cultural appreciation, a level of knowledge and perspective and a capability to communicate are **all** being included in measuring the effectiveness of special education programs. **Well**...while it's true that artificial barriers of overprotection and underexpectations can magnify either the gifted or handicapped students problems, this all seems a little ambitious. Inappropriate expectations in either direction are barriers to information and learning for students who don't learn in the usual way.

Microcomputers are a real breakthrough in communication enhancement for those students who need adaptations and alternatives, whether it's changing text to speech, braille, visual modeling, or whatever. Computers can bring special students out of their shell in a soothing and personalized manner. They are adding to the adaptation repertoire of special education teaching—capitalizing on strengths and remediating weaknesses. They should also encourage the affective development by incorporating both coping and social skills. But it is important to take a considered approach to using computers—stepping back and considering how plans for using computers can help reach educational goals.

Highly Trained Professionals—The Key to Getting the Job Done

After several generations of educational neglect, recent reform efforts have had a subtle but real effect on teachers. Special educators must now know how to coordinate medical, guidance, and social work disciplines. To institute educational reforms requires that education issues be kept before the public. Promoting public awareness and activating available resources is essential to enhanced opportunities and stimulating employment for both our gifted and our handicapped students. But we should be equally concerned about how to get their teachers through the same doorway.

In teacher shortage states (New Jersey, Texas, and California are just three examples), there is a new type of quick and easy **emergency teacher certification** that affects special educators. Special education teachers are called upon to expand their skills, update knowledge, and reorient all teachers to teach mainstreamed students differently. At the same time society is placing greater responsibilities on special educators, we are getting untrained **emergency teachers** for students with special needs. In states experiencing shortages, we are getting teachers in special needs classrooms that have had neither training in special needs, classrooms, or anything remotely connected to education. Los Angeles, for example, is not only recruiting in other countries, but has placed ads in national newspapers soliciting applications from **anyone** interested in teaching. One wonder what the hue and cry would be if we were getting emergency physicians or other professionals. Particularly if personnel shortages were coupled with great advances in technological aids, increased responsibility to reach out to other professionals, and expectations that **they** had to improve identification, diagnosis, and remediation. And, on top of all this, they had to motivate those involved to participate.

USING SOME OF THE FIRST PRACTICAL APPLICATION PROGRAMS FROM ARTIFICIAL INTELLIGENCE RESEARCH TO MAKE SOMETHING HAPPEN FOR HISPANIC AND ESL STUDENTS

Minority students have often looked on education a little like a rainy day: boring, a big problem, uncontrollable, to be adjusted to, and impossible to get through dry. A recent national study sees Hispanic students being **wasted** by the schools.[1] Nearly 40 percent of Hispanic students drop out before they start high school. And less than half complete the normal high school program. Is there a hidden curriculum that shuts these students out of open stocks of knowledge? Projected to be the country's largest minority by 1990, we are failing these and other students, who do not have English as a first language (ESL students), in vast numbers.

[1] National Commission on Secondary Schooling for Hispanics, "Make Something Happen." Washington, D.C., Hispanic Policy Development Project, 1984. Copies of the report are available from the Hispanic Policy Development Project, 1001 Connecticut Avenue, N.W., Washington, D.C. 20036.

Figure 12. Computer Composite Image.

Not developing a social sensitivity in the students who have English as their native language compounds the failure. The school system simply reinforces the social relations already in place in American society. As ESL children are pushed out of the educational mainstream, students who have English as their native language are losing the opportunity for being exposed to the significance of cultural similarities and differences. There is a great deal of research support for the educational usefulness of group work and interlanguage talk (between ESL and native language students) in the second language classroom. It is through such multiple cultural encounters that children gain an understanding of the nature of our pluralistic society as well as insight into their own values, customs and identities.

Why are we losing such a large percentage of ESL students and what can be done to reverse this trend? Many of these children lack a sound base in language and reading skills which prevents them from achieving their goals. And without fluency in the English language, they are cut off from many educational and occupational futures. In addition, numerous Hispanic students do not have close personal contact in school with adults who care about their aspirations and futures.

What seems to be needed is increased opportunity within the school setting to gain a firm base in their native language. Yet there is a contradiction between national programs that call for English to be the dominant language in ESL instruction and research which suggests that students must be familiar with their first language to be fully successful in the second. If bilingual programs prove to be politically unacceptable, or if we don't have the resources to get the job done, new developments in artificial intelligence may help us reach some of the same goals. Unilingual English teachers can, for example, use some of the recently developed AI tools to teach Spanish as a "foreign" language—from preschool on. This gives us the opportunity for open and undistorted communication among equals.

Artificial Intelligence Technologies That Bring ESL Students into the Learning Process

A first step is to provide motivating oral and visual learning activities in both English and Spanish through a kind of spontaneous apprenticeship with others and with machine intelligence. The Kurzweil scanner is an example of an AI device that can read, speak, infer and store in its memory stories in several languages. This can provide a bridge linking the book, different languages, videoscreen, and the human mind. The machine uses an advanced optical scanner to bring information to a reading/speaking program that was developed by artificial intelligence researchers.[2] The machine can reach back through the corridors of time to historical information stored (in several languages) in traditional books. Cheaper scanners, like the Omni-Reader (Oberon International

[2] The Reading Computer, developed by Kurzweil Computer Products Inc., Cambridge, MA (A division of the Xerox Corporation).

Inc.), attach to Apple and IBM microcomputers and can transfer print to the computer's electronic system faster than any typist.[3]

A much cheaper program is also sold for the Apple II computer. "Text-to-Speech:65" is a translation program for the SSi-263 speech synthesizer (that is connected to the Apple.) Rather than scanning the book and reading automatically, this program requires having the text already on a computer program—or having it typed from the computer keyboard (which goes directly into speech). The "Text-to-Speech:65" is compatible with the "Sonix:65 Speech Operating System" and "Phonetic Speech Editor." When an ESL student can both see and hear the word, the learning process is more dynamic. This software will also work with a SynPhonix 100 speech synthesizer on the Apple II series computer. If there are words that are frequently mispronounced by the translator, it is possible to manually set them up on an "Exception Table" which overrides the translation rules.

Another cheap language translator has been bought out by SE&A Product Development Corporation of Glendale, CA. Their hand-held electronic device converts English words into their foreign equivalents and emits them in a human-like synthesized voice that "speaks" with the proper accent. Called "World-Walker, the Talking Translator," it is a bit larger than a pocket calculator, and is available in modules that convert English into Spanish, German, French or Japanese—or vice versa.

Teachers can also use Apple computers to teach foreign languages with multi-lingual computer programs. These programs put out by the Professor Corporation, Ft. Lauderdale, FL, allow for the entry of text in Spanish, French, German, Danish/Norwegian, Finnish/Swedish, Hawaiian, Hungarian, Italian, Latin/Dutch, Portuguese, Turkish and Czech. "The Great Creator" is a multi-lingual multiple-choice, true/false and fill-in-the-blank questionnaire generator. And the "Multi-Lingual Language Teacher" has a library of drawings in color as an aid for teaching "foreign" languages. Either teachers or students can create and operate their own programs for language instruction. The publishers also offer "Multi-Lingual Criss-Cross Word," "Multi-Lingual Word Maze" and "Multi-Lingual Word Game."[4]

---

[3] "Text-to-Speech:65." Artic Technologies, Auburn Heights, MI.

[4] The Professor, Ft. Lauderdale, FL.

Using Recent Advances in Artificial Intelligence to Build a Sound Language Base

In the early grades, it is important for students to gain a firm base in their native language. Reading the printed word requires that children learn to associate spoken words with their corresponding written forms. Rhyming one syllable words gives students a chance to play with letter-sound (grapheme-phoneme) relationships in both languages. Children who have English as their second language should become sensitive to these features of spoken and written languages before they learn to read. Using the new AI technology, like the Reading Computer that reads to children in both languages, can help unilingual English teachers provide this necessary background in a child's first language.

The Reading Computer, built by a subsidiary of Xerox, is one of the first practical uses of artificial intelligence—a type of "expert" or "knowledge-based" system. It can scan texts in the language you choose, make linguistic inferences and reads to a student via voice synthesizing device. Children see and hear the printed word in the desired language and make the connection to visual images and higher level thinking skills. They see, hear, speak and sometimes arrange the words in a creative context.

The system contains a knowledge base and a reasoning component to process symbols rather than numbers. The knowledge base not only contains facts (like a database) but operating rules based on that knowledge. The Reading Computer has "visual" capabilities which enable it to read various languages and recognize almost any typeface. It can make psycholinguistic inferences with a high degree of accuracy. There is a dictionary and a parallel set of rules for pronunciation which allows it to read at a rate of 250 words per minute. Students have control over the reading process and are able to adjust the rate of speech—as well as the sound of the speaking voice. They can also instruct the computer to go back and reread specified sections. Although the reading computers are specific machines with their own sets of specialized programs, it is possible to access the information they contain with a regular microcomputer (any distance away) either by direct connection or telephone lines.

Other artificial intelligence programs are being worked on that will expand the teaching and learning of foreign languages. Grants from the Annenberg/CPB Project have been given to MIT and Brown University to develop sophisticated language education programs. MIT is applying computers, videodisc and interactive audio technology to language learning. With the help of discoveries in artificial intelligence, they are developing a natural conversational method of language teaching as opposed to the drill centered approach commonly used. Brown is investigating ways to make abstract concepts more concrete and visual. Their project provides an electronic information exchange incorporating human reactions in problem solving contexts.

Artificial Intelligence—The Notion of Putting Together Hardware and Programs to Create New "Thinking" Entities

It is fine to speak of using some of the first practical applications of artificial intelligence research to insure that Hispanic students are not left out of the educational process. But briefly, what is artificial intelligence? Quite simply, it is putting a certain reasoning process on an electronic microchip and/or into a computer disk or other storage device. These programs have a set of rules and understandings that are built on inferential knowledge. They draw their responses from formulas that represent some human expertise—from language translation to medical diagnosis. Containing both factual knowledge and, to a degree, the knowledge of good human judgment, these programs reason, use an inference procedure and utilize information—whether printed text or the spoken word. The example we emphasize here, reading/speaking machines, read various typeset by performing an accurate kind of psycholinguistic guessing game and converting the printed material into fairly clear speech.

These and other knowledge-based systems are just beginning to come onto the microcomputer market. Some give expert advice on everything from administration and learning to problem diagnosis and suggestions for remediation. Only the first artificially intelligent learning systems are available today. Soon we will see a new wave of these innovative learning products as AI programs come to gradually touch every aspect of how our students learn reading and language arts.

Using the Dynamic Capabilities of Computer-Based Technology to Create a Highly Stimulating Environment

The primary cause of the failure of ESL students to acquire sound language skills in English is not the lack of innate ability. Rather, we view it as a failure in institutional methodology and motivational techniques. Relying on extra drill and practice and rote skill training has not been successful for the bulk of ESL students. Likewise, simply using computerized learning tools to replicate boring practice lessons provides little payoff. Using interactive AI computer programs like the Reading Machine or OZ[5] to connect these same programs can amplify language communication found at school, in peer group situations and at home. In fact, some of these computer-based tools may help bring parents and teachers into a cooperative relationship that revolves around technology and a rich language heritage.

Too much of what is taught in school is for school purpose—not life or higher educational purpose. The actual utility of what is taught is the best kept secret in education. Too frequently, neither the teacher nor the student are let in on that confidential information. The new technology should not simply be used to extend the institutional mistakes of the past. What is viewed as hazy or irrelevant to ESL students in an earlier technological base (like the workbook) remains so in another. AI programs serve as one valid alternative to using computers as electronic worksheets or to simply teaching "computer literacy." Not only can they give learners access to information about what they are learning, but why they are learning it.

The earliest possible use of these new technological tools is crucial since we lost nearly half of our Hispanic students before they complete junior high school. To cut into what is the highest drop out rate of any minority group and help bridge the language and cultural differences between the home and school—as well as learning problems raised by lack of motivation—we now have available to us the most powerful learning tool ever invented—artificial intelligence. It can serve as a collaborator and a motivator that allows us to do for many what was done for a few. And the benefits will go to all our students.

AI language programs can create a stimulating micro environment that focuses on the individual talents of the student. Higher order thinking skills and systematic problem solving strategies go hand-in-hand with the technology. Artificially intelligent machines, like the Reading Computer, create an exciting language arts environment. These electronic learning tools can serve as a multiethnic bridge to build respect across cultures. Children can use "intelligent" work stations to listen,

[5] OZ: Management Control. Fox & Geller, Inc., 604 Market Street, Elmwood Park, NJ 07407

respond, record and continually interact with two languages—and two sets of children's literature and social values. The bilingual support these AI language programs could give to most of our classrooms, which have unilingual English teachers, is not inconsequential.

The Value of Multicultural Education to Our Nation

The educational failure of minorities is an old malignancy in America—if it's not "biological destiny," it's "excellence." No matter how sincere, the result is the same—minority students not only become culturally dependent, but fail. And majority students are deprived of the sense of social sensitivity that only close multicultural contact can bring. Fortunately, we now have some computer-based tools that have some potential for bringing parents and teachers into a cooperative relationship revolving around technology and a rich language/ethnic heritage. Bilingual students are a scarce resource for the renewal of foreign language training and multicultural education. The issue should not only be how quickly to absorb non-Anglo speaking children into the dominant culture, but how the mastery of two languages and cultures can have special benefits for the student and for the United States as a whole.

Differing views on cultural and linguistic diversity are really what's behind the debate over bilingual education. Yet the multicultural mix of the United States is seen by many as a driving force behind the dynamic creativity of our country. This mix of race and culture is part of the reason why we have over 125 Nobel Prize winners (with individuals from a range of American cultural groups) while a unicultural country like Japan has a total of two. We should celebrate and utilize the cultural diversity that has given us a creative mix that has the potential technological leadership on an international level. Why push aside the very students that can help us continue this process?

Artificially intelligent programs can create a stimulating micro environment that focuses on the individual talents of the Hispanic student. And higher order thinking skills and systematic problem solving strategies go hand-in-hand with the technology. If these systems can make even a dent in one of our crucial institutions for affecting minority poverty schools—then the result is not insignificant. If poverty becomes a minority dominated condition, then we will all be poorer.

AI machines like the Reading Computer create an exciting language arts environment. These electronic learning tools can serve as a multiethnic bridge to build respect across cultures. Teachers and schools have to show more concern about cultures and language differences. It is, after all, the teacher's attitude that is the key factor.

The Future: Out of the Artificial Intelligence Lab and into the Multicultural Language Classroom

The Reading Computer is simply one of the first examples of how "artificially intelligent" computer "knowledge systems" can be used by children to associate with more than one language heritage. When this technology is used to amplify human multicultural contacts, we have a tool that allows ESL students to develop self-concept and a sense of identity. And, at least as importantly, allows ENL students to understand that people who belong to cultural groups other than their own are real people with needs, feelings and emotions similar to their own.

New technological developments allow all our students to interact with the products of the imaginations of other cultures in a highly motivating and respectful way. Having "foreign" language instruction (in Spanish for Hispanic students) and a multicultural component in the curriculum has few political opponents. And although education is a form of politics, there is no social or political reason why Hispanic students can't be allowed a more solid base in their rich cultural and language heritage. Students who have English as their first language can likewise be afforded the chance to gain a heightened sensitivity to other cultural themes, norms and social change.

Knowledge-based AI computer systems is a new technology with enough power to alter the dynamics and fabric of the educational system. But the nature and extent of that alteration remains open. We must make choices that impel the technology along a useful path. It always comes back to our discipline, the more we understand pedagogically, the better the path we will choose in this uncertain technological predicament. Our choices today will shape our educational and social futures. Latent in the new technology is the possibility of providing educational futures for all that were once possible for only the few.

CHAPTER 6

EVALUATING SOFTWARE

USERS AS CRITICS

IN "THE BEGINNING," way back in 1980, the few schools that had a microcomputer were happy to get any private or public domain software thrown their way. Evaluating the few programs that they were fortunate enough to get their hands on was the least of their concerns. By the "Dark Ages" of educational computing, 1982, schools were getting a few programs that were included with the computer, borrowing from the local computer store, and ordering by direct mail. Documentation (instructions) were crude or non-existant and product support didn't really exist. But there was a growing awareness that they should. Many of the programs were of the old drill and practice variety. They relied on rote learning and took people out of the process; negatively affecting critical and creative thinking.

By 1983 many products were no longer dull, but the bulk of the software simply didn't teach much. There were a few exceptions in the area of simulation (like **Oregon Trail**), word processing (like **Bank Street Writer**), and electronic spread sheets (for developing mathematical models). In addition to better quality, we were finally getting some good product reviews.

By 1984-85 we had good extensions of the best products, new peripherals (like the Koala pad), and a flood of new programs. The old concern that there wasn't **any** good software was no longer valid. Most importantly, many teachers were no longer afraid of having computers in the classroom—and they were taking charge of program selection. By 1986 it was impossible for most teachers to avoid educational computing. The major problem now is how to systematically integrate some of the good courseware into the classroom.

Starting Points

Software reviews are now available in every issue of dozens of journals (see chart). In fact, we are now suffering from a software evaluation glut and it is nearly impossible for the teacher, acting alone, to sort out what is useful for her classroom. Students can help by sifting through some of the software evaluations. They can learn a great deal by doing computer program reviews along **book report** lines. In districts that haven't selected the hardware, software should be considered first. But most schools now have the hardware in place and the teachers have been given the responsibility for choosing, much like selecting what films they want their class to see. However, before this evaluation process can begin teachers have to figure out how to get the equipment up and running so that they, or their student reviewers, can "test drive" the software programs.

After learning the basics of how to turn the computer on and load a program, teachers can quickly check to see if the flow makes sense. If they have time, they can try the program as they think a successful or unsuccessful student might. What happens when mistakes are made? Is it more fun to fail than to succeed?

There are time consuming evaluation issues surrounding the multitude of software programs to be dealt with. Whether it's a simulation, Logo microworlds, word processing, spreadsheets, database managers, expert (AI) systems or getting the computer in contact with the outside world (telecommunications) through a modem/software combination. Whew! That's quite a universe to be familiar with. Without students taking some of the responsibility the task is becoming almost insurmountable.

The most interesting way to approach the software evaluation process is like approaching a book or a movie review. Like book or movie critics, similar points tend to run through various evaluations; even though the process is very subjective and personal. Some teachers may find particular courseware motivating and easy to integrate into their instructional program—others may disagree. The bottom line for the teacher is do you like it, and do at least some of your students like it?

Teachers' personalities, character, values, and motivations also have a direct relationship with the development of a computer assisted curriculum. In an informal survey of classroom teachers we found that those most familiar with computers were also the teachers most excited about educational computing. Familiarity seemed to breed positive attitudes toward evaluating software, modifying existing programs, and incorporating computer-based instruction into their instructional plans. The small percentage of teachers who indicated that they were very familiar with educational computing felt that it was possible for microcomputer courseware to stand side by side with books as important instructional tools. Like books, programs were viewed as good, bad, and indifferent. In fact, many of the evaluation techniques used with print materials were also successfully applied to computer software.

Figure 13. Computer Generated Image.

The Role of the Teacher and the Student in Choosing Software

The computer has the potential of being the most authoritarian controlling device ever invented. It also has the potential to draw students and teachers closer together in a manner that implies shared ownership over the curriculum.

With hundreds of samples to choose from (floppy disks are sometimes even included in magazines) teachers couldn't possibly sample everything themselves. Why not let children take some responsibility for their learning?

Children are capable of more penetrating evaluative thinking and intensive inquiry than is normally allowed for in school. The upper elementary grade teachers we worked with had a great deal of success having their students assist in software evaluation. The child's view is an important consideration. After all, the program must make sense to the child. The whole evaluation process can be turned into an excellent learning experience for groups of children. Having students help construct elements of the learning process can even assist us in building a framework for incorporating other aspects of the curriculum.

Curriculum is a cooperative and interactive venture to relate experience to intellectual/emotional development. On both an individual and social level those directly involved with the process must be taken seriously. Working together they can decide what benefits are gained from particular software programs. After all, the software **user** is in the best position to decide if the program is taking people out of the process—or whether learners are in control of the computers, rather than vice versa. Without question, teachers and students are the ones who experience the consequences of these choices. And they are the ones who most quickly learn the consequences of poor choices.

Some Practical Specifics That the Teacher Can Build into the Evaluation Process

The same criteria that are applied to other instructional materials can be applied to evaluating educational computing courseware. The following list is an example:

1. Does the software meet the memory and attention span demands of your students?
2. Can the courseware be modified to meet individual learning requirements?
3. Can it be adjusted to the learning style of the user?
4. Education is an increasingly visual process. Are the aesthetics and graphics (visual processing) dynamic and appropriate?
5. Does the software make use of the unique qualities of the computer?
6. Does it meet instructional objectives—and is it educationally sound?
7. Are higher order thinking skills involved in the computer lesson?
8. Can the children understand the language level?
9. Does the courseware give appropriate feedback?
10. Does the software free the teacher for more rewarding and challenging teaching?

Evaluating software does not have to be a long tedious task when students are enlisted in the process. Here is a sample student courseware evaluation checklist that we have found helpful.

STUDENT SOFTWARE EVALUATION ACTIVITY

Student's Name ____________________
Names of other students who used the program with you ____________________
Program Name ____________________ Subject ____________________
Publisher ____________________

How much time did the program take? ________ minutes
What type of program was it? (Check one)
____ game ____ simulation ____ spreadsheet ____ drill and practice
____ test ____ telecommunications ____ expert system
____ problem solving ____ word processing ____ other____________________

1. Did you need help using this program? ____ yes ____ no

Check the response that you think best tells about the program.

2. The directions were: ____ great ____ good ____ O.K.____ poor ____ bad
3. The program was easy to read: ____ very ____ somewhat ____ difficult
4. The graphics were: ____ great ____ good ____ O.K. ____ poor ____ bad
5. The sound was: ____ great ____ good ____ O.K. ____ poor ____ bad
6. Was the program easy to use? ____ yes ____ no ____ kind of difficult

Comments: ____________________

7. What happens when you do something wrong? ____________________
8. What happens when you do things correctly? ____________________
9. Did the program really get you involved? ____ yes ____ no ____ somewhat
10. Were you able to choose what happened in the program? ____________________
11. What was the most interesting part of the program? ____________________
____
12. Was the program helpful to you? ____ yes ____ no____ somewhat
13. How did you do? What did you accomplish? ____________________
____
14. What did you like best about the program? ____________________
____
15. What grade would you give the program? ____ A ____ B ____ C ____ D ____ F
16. What did you like least? ____________________
____
17. Would you recommend this program to a friend? ____ yes ____ no
Why or why not? ____________________

Extended Activity

Choose one of the following:

– Write a news report about an event or incident in the program.
– Write or dramatize a T.V. interview with the main character.
– Review the program for a magazine.

- —Make up a student guide for the program. Use your own directions and illustrations.
- —Create a game using characters from the program or the program itself.
- —Interview other students who have used the program and write down their responses.
- —Create your own graphics or draw a picture about your favorite part of the program.

Moving Through Stages of Educational Computing

Information and communication about a new technology seem to be key elements for moving through stages of knowledge about how an innovation works. From decisions about how to adopt or reject the innovation—to implementation on a widespread basis—to refinement.

Educational computing has evolved from 1980. There is a diminishing need for drill and practice software. Except for those generations who left school before computers became a common instructional tool, computer literacy is also receding as a courseware concern. To make the most effective use of human electronic tool partnerships educators must learn to sift the good software programs from the mediocre. Computer courseware development must pay attention to formative evaluation. As educators become conscious of the quality of software, companies are being forced into a field testing and revision cycle.

Financially, the good news is that more useful software is rapidly becoming available (at a decreased cost). The bad news is that schools are finding more excellent software than they can afford to purchase. There is some public domain (free) software developed under various public sector grants, but this is becoming less important as times goes on.

It is the job of the publishing company to sell programs. The companies themselves, the professional organizations, including teachers and students are all resources that can help in the evaluation process. But, in the final analysis, it comes down to the teacher knowing enough about learning and the characteristics of effective instruction to make instructional judgements about computer courseware. Once teachers have become aware of the possibilities and drawbacks of educational computing software everyone should step back and trust the teacher to teach and the child to learn.

Educational Computing Journals

This is a sampling of the educational computing journals that carry reviews on software evaluation.

AEDS Journal
Arithmetic Teacher
Art Education
Classroom Computer Learning
Classroom Computer News
Computers and Education
Computer Education
Computers in the Schools
Computers, Reading and Language Arts
The Computing Teacher
Creative Computing
Educational Computer
Educational Technology
Educational Computer Magazine
Electronic Education
Electronic Learning
Journal of Computer-Based Instruction
Journal of Computers in Science and Mathematics
Journal of Educational Technology Systems
Mathematics Teacher
Microcomputers in Education
Tech Trends
Technological Horizons in Education

SELECTING SOFTWARE

When selecting software it is important to look beyond the colorful graphics and catchy sound effects. The list of suggestions that follow are designed to assist in the software and courseware selection process.

Identify the skills involved in the program. If the software fails to develop skills relevant to your instructional objectives it is of limited value.

Check the program's correlation to other curricular areas and activities. Can you extend the courseware beyond the limited computer application?

Look for programs that supply multiple and varied cues to the user. Is the program too repetitive? Is there diversity and multiple modes of presentation?

Select programs that foster active student involvement. Remember that the quality of involvement is as important as the quantity.

Seek out programs that promote personal and social growth. Programs that offer violence and social and sexual stereotyping have no legitimate place in educational programming.

Select programs which are appropriate for the intended audience. A well designed piece of software does not overwhelm its user with complex directions or confusing directives. Select software with children's preferences and interests in mind as well as level of difficulty.

Seek out courseware that accomodates a range of proficiencies. Programs written for a single skill level are not as desirable as those that embrace a broader audience. Some students may not find it challenging while others may be overwhelmed at its complexity. Many computer games have adopted this strategy with success.

Select programs that can be used by more than one student. Children prefer computer activities that allow for interaction with classmates. The social interaction is an important learning tool. In addition, many teachers have limited computer resources and access. Software that allows for group use can increase the availability and build new communication links between students.

Select programs that fit into your time frame. Programs that exceed the available class period can often pose problems. Many programs do not accomodate multiple users and the student who uses the program next automatically picks up the former student's unfinished activity.

Check the documentation. Are the directions clear and easy to understand? Is there a teacher and student manual? Is the documentation incorporated into the program itself? Does the program offer on-line help?

Experiment with all of the available options before selecting the software. Make mistakes. Deliberately hit the wrong key. Press the return key at an incorrect time and see what happens.

Check for hardware compatibility. Some programs require more than one disk drive, extended memory capacities, or special peripherals. Most companies list the required accessories, but if it is not clearly specified, consult the publisher before making your decision.

Some Questions Regarding Software

In coping with software evaluation, teachers need to deal with the following questions regarding computer programs.

1. Is the software interactive? Does it take advantage of the computer's strengths?
2. Is there sufficient and appropriate feedback?
3. Is the program able to stand alone without a lot of teacher input and directives?
4. Does the program fit into the instructional scheme of the overall curriculum plan?
5. Is the program able to be adapted to meet individual needs?
6. Will the program save the teacher time?
7. Does the program allow for student creativity and innovation?
8. Does the program wait to act on a command (allowing the student to think about an answer)?
9. What kind of teaching-learning style is modeled?

The usefulness of any computer program cannot be evaluated in isolation. A program's effectiveness and quality must be judged with an application in mind. Remember too, that in the final analysis, you are the one who has to use it with your class of students, the real question is: **Do you like it**?

SIMULATION GAMES

Fortunately this was not the ultimate flawed lift-off contingency, requiring the Range Safety Officer to completely destroy the shuttle. High explosives were built in during construction and wired with special radio receivers that monitor the shuttle's ascent. If the projected point of impact was a populated area, a signal would be sent and the shuttle and crew would be vaporized. At least they were beyond that ugly possibility. But the space shuttle crew knew there were serious problems as they climbed higher in space and out over the Atlantic. Now they were in trouble—complete engine failure. The astronauts called the emergency landing site (the computer) and started to descend. They were headed for the strip in Sengal, West Africa. Having no engine power to draw on, they glided in toward the 10,000 foot landing site set aside for emergency situations. To this point the astronauts had been too busy to be scared, but as the African site grew larger before their eyes they realized they would crash short of the runway. Then they heard mission control, "Well, let's try it again." The view out of their windshield blinked, and they were back to 10,000 feet, ready for another practice of the emergency scenario.

Had this been a real emergency landing, the astronauts would have died in the crash, and the space shuttle would have been two billion dollars worth of debris. Fortunately, this was a computer simulation. The shuttle's flying characteristics, sounds, sights, and gravitational load were produced to the extent that the astronauts say the simulator flies just like the shuttle. When the space shuttle really did have its first engine failure, the crew reported being surprised at how similar the whole thing felt to the simulation.

Besides designing test flights for the pilots, engineers are trying out new systems to see how they will perform in real-life situations. The space shuttle simulator also has a computer program that can mimic the maneuvers of a new generation of jets and other aircraft. A computer synthesizer monitors and traces even subtle sounds like air flow. Three-dimensional computer graphics recreates reality from each window. The space shuttle runway, down to the last bump, is exactly like that of Dakar, the Kennedy Space Center, or Edwards Air Force Base. Visibility can be changed from very clear to heavy fog and from day to night. Even a little air turbulence or a flat tire can be thrown in for good measure. A system failure or a mistake in judgement, however, does not result in a gory graphics finish. Rather, they just push a button and start again.

By these standards computer-based educational simulation is now very primitive. However, connecting to higher computer memories, speed, graphics, and reasoning—and the essential ingredient of better software—makes for powerful educational experiences. In fact, simulations are perhaps the most exciting part of computer learning and have incredible potential.

We already have microcomputer simulation programs that allow users to benefit from artificial intelligence products. Until very recently a larger computer was needed to use a reasoning program that provided definition and possible solutions to simulated real world problems. Intellicorp's **Knowledge Engineering Environment** is just one example of a microcomputer program that pinpoints trouble and automatically tests a variety of corrective actions. These AI development tools can diagnose real or simulated problems, learn to improve the probability of correct diagnosis, and even produce suggestions for solutions.

Combining Word Processing and Simulation

Detective is an adventure game that actually allows students to write part of the simulation. Evidence appears, and disappears on the screen if a player does not reason quickly enough. Simulation is combined with writing on the computer; and at the push of a button, students get a perfect copy of their detective story.

Meteorologists at the National Weather Service are now using three dimensional computer simulations to create a synthesis of satellite, weather stations and aircraft data—and project that data into the future. Using a computer simulator, three dimensional images can be projected onto a two dimensional surface (such as a computer screen) for a given time period in the future.

An educational simulation uses a real-life model that allows the student to enter control data. One microcomputer simulation lets the student operate a nuclear power plant. The student operator is faced with the problem of producing as much energy as possible while dealing with emergency situations based on real events like the Three Mile Island disaster. The program even allows for increasing the risk factor by placing the reactor in an area prone to earthquakes.

Other simulation programs deal with chemical reactions too dangerous to allow in the classroom. Some simulations are constructed so that the user is allowed to go back in history. Students can participate, but may not change the direction of historical events.

Oregon Trail is a simulation carefully built on the actual diaries of early Oregon settlers. **Pioneers** are given a map on the video screen and a set of decisions to make in moving across the country. Although it does not exactly replicate a particular trip, it has compiled a model of all the trips during a five year period of time. With good graphics and accurate information on which to base their decisions, they try to make their way to Oregon. Like the real pioneers, not all students are successful. This is an excellent group activity, but students may choose to work in pairs or as individuals.

A simulation is only one representation of reality. However, the same thing could be said of many books. The teacher must be sensitive to all these factors and be able to use the computer simulation as a jumping off point for discussing the full reality.

Any simulation is a presentation of simplified representations. Simulation models may actually mimic physical models (as with the space shuttle); use print to create a concept (**Detective** is a good example); or like **Oregon Trail**, combine the two based on a mathematical model of the relationship in the system.

Simulations are a method for representing, understanding, and solving interdependent problems. They can give us new insights about the past, present, and future as well as provide us with a new tool for studying everything from economic activity to physical and social behavior. The World Bank and the United Nations, for example, are now using simulations to predict world population growth.

When simulations are combined with powerful computer graphics, they become a potent device for imparting information in ways print and pictures never could. This holds exciting potential for educational applications. The $1,000 a second, price of computerized moving pictures that make up some of the commercials that we see on TV are dropping rapidly. It will soon be a financially approachable medium for instructional use. The possibilities for presenting concepts, formerly thought of as too abstract (in mathematics, biology, physics, architecture, and art, for example) are now being re-examined.

The capability of making abstract concepts more concrete is only one avenue being explored. High resolution moving graphics can be used to display and create movies. Students may start with a picture on the computer, but the realistic computer-generated pictures that follow

Figure 14. Computer Composite Image.

could take them forward or backward in history and generate a whole scene based on one painting, pictures of the past, or an artist's conception of the future.

MIT researchers have also designed a device that allows the user to "drive" down the street of a modern city. Whichever way the student decides to turn, a realistic image of that street is computer generated.

With databases becoming more accessible, simulations can be broadcast across telephone lines, or played over the air like CB radios. Telecommunication networks allow students to interact with simulations between schools, cities, or even countries.

FIRMS ABANDON THE SCHOOL MARKET

IBM seems to have decided to leave the school market to Apple, with Tandy (Radio Shack), Commodore, and Atari making a few inroads. IBM's main school vehicle, the PCjr. will undoubtly be **serviced** for the next five years, or more. And even outdated Texas Instruments machines can be productively turned over to one or two specific services; like word processing or programming. The problem is that there will be less and less educational software for computers made by companies that are pulling back from the school market. The result will be more educational programs for the solidly entrenched Apple and fewer for the IBM PCjr. It's surprising that a firm as influential as IBM has done such damage to its credibility as a reliable supplier to the school market. Unless IBM has a change of heart, worries less about high profit margins, and announces a new school oriented product, they may fade from the instructional classroom picture.

What can schools do about the uncertainties of the computer market? Waiting for new models is a little like waiting for new cars before teaching driver's education. Sure they are different and have more power for the energy expended, but there is only so long you can wait to teach a student ready to learn to drive. You have to take some of the models available and put students behind the wheel.

Use of Computer Software

There is still the element of the frontier in educational computing. But recently we have seen cooperative agreements between publishers and educators that are designed to discourage illegal copying—without locking up programs in ways that prevent the teacher from making changes. When programs are copy protected, it is usually impossible to change it around to fit individual classroom situations, add speech, or make a back-up copy.

The Home is Surpassing the School as a Consumer of Educational Software

The boundaries between instructional and entertainment software, and between home and school are becoming blurred. The home has now surpassed the school as the primary puchaser of instructional software. This means that publishers are aiming for a different market. The communication gap between schools and publishers continues to expand at the very time schools are getting microcomputers in quantity.

Another event is also hurting educational computing; a computer industry "shakeout." Industry expansion continues to expand, but at a reduced rate—10 percent instead of 30 percent per year. Computers may be booming in schools, but the industry situation is a little like the auto industry's early days when over a thousand different producers were reduced to a dozen. We bought more cars, but there were fewer companies making a profit on them.

Our 1985-86 "Best Seller List" for Educational Software

Kids on Keys (Spinnaker)
Mind Prober (Human Edge)
Birdbreed (EduTech)
Early Games for Children (Springboard)
Master Type (Scarborough)
Word Attack (Davidson and Associates)
The Incredible Laboratory (Sunburst)
Kindercomp (Spinnaker)
Adventures in Flesh (Krell Software Company)
Success with Math (CBS)
Simpolicon: Simulation of Political and Economic Development (Cross Cultural Software)
Facemaker (Spinnaker)
Homeword (Sierra On-Line Inc.)
Typing Tutor III (Simon & Schuster)
Bank Street Story Book (Mindscape)
Koala Painter (Koala Technologies)

Think Tank (Living Videotext)
M-I-S-S-I-N-G L-I-N-K-S: Young People's Literature (Sunburst)
The Print Shop (Broderbund Software)

CHAPTER 7

NEW DIGITIZED LITERACIES: MIXING VISUAL MEDIA, THE ARTS, PRINT AND COMPUTER-BASED TECHNOLOGY

SCHOOLS ARE NOT equipped to keep pace with the dramatic automation and integration of the fine arts and the new technology. To retain their role in the learning process the school, in cooperation with the institutions (including the home and the media), must be in on the creation of new art forms—containing both technology and fine arts. The current tendency in some circles is to concentrate on strictly technical problems—when it's really the human principles underlying the technology that are most important.

The fine arts and computer controlled technology are inexorably mixed. The intellectual tools provided by the humanities may very well be more useful for dealing with the technology of the future than the narrow band of linear skills being presented under the guise of high technology. Already computers like the Apple Macintosh, are making use of a broad band of visual imagery skills—and new computers will continue to add a rich array of intellectual styles to their operation. High tech developments have often gone hand-in-hand with ideas that play to our humanness. The fact that television and the human potential movement grew up together was not simply coincidence. As high technology creeps into our lives there is a high touch reaction to it. Just as the birth control pill brought more flexibility to women's lives and changed lifestyles and marriage styles, today's technology is changing the way we think about ourselves—everything from looking at sleep as "clearing the program," to serving as computer-based metaphors for thinking, to microprocessors acting as a controlling device in automobile carburetors. Advances in technology almost seem to force a "high touch" renaissance for the humanities; this in turn leads to technology taking on some of the characteristics of our humanness. New computers are using visual images, speech and even movement to move beyond linear typing skills—interacting with information, concepts and people. Future computers will, in varying degrees, require not only the narrow range of linguistic and mathematical skills we are now teaching in schools but visual, artistic, musical, interpersonal and movement skills (as for example, dance).

It was, after all, computer controlled technology that allowed more people access to Shakespearean Theater, in one night of television, than in the previous 500 years of live theater. This is just one example of how technology can assist in bringing the arts to people that would otherwise

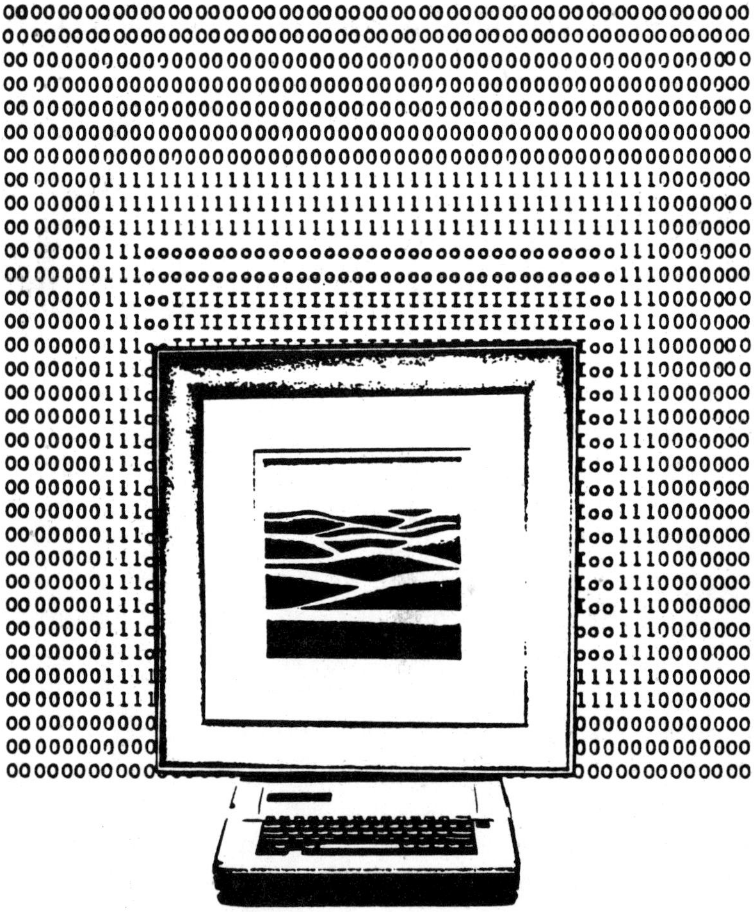

Figure 15. Computer Composite Image.

never be exposed to such "high touch" influences. Of course the flip side of this coin is that intelligent TV viewing is the exception rather than the rule—we can also be distracted from literature and the arts. The same television brings us banal preachers asking for social security checks, wrestling with Cowboy Bob, "Attack of the Full Figured Gals" (the Playboy Channel), music videos, violence, game shows, irresponsible liquor ads, and other lowest common denominator impediments to knowledge. The broad educational possibilities are usually left out of media discussions—the emphasis being projecting images, whether true or false, tawdry or tasteful. And more often than not it mixes all of these image possibilities together in a manner that allows only the most visually literate of the viewers to sort out the real from the unreal and the mentally expanding from the intellectually deadening.

Digitization of the Medium

Much of television production and broadcasting relies on computer-based devices in which microprocessing chips are embedded (including recording, broadcasting and satellite technology). Soon we will have digital television receivers with computer controlled pictures and sound systems providing greater clarity, color and possibilities for interaction. The technology is also bringing us into an era of narrow casting that can provide us with varying degrees of human choice. The VCR cassette tape is the ultimate in narrow casting—providing everything from golf lessons with Jack Nicklaus to exercising with Jane Fonda.

The merger of formally different areas of human understanding makes possible an electronic skinner box that can be illusory in relation to real human space. We see digitized page turns on the evening news, faces spinning on globes, fish turning into butterflies, and animated motorcyclists making 90 degree turns that violate the laws of physics (in the movie **TRON**, for example). Clean space on the video screen or printer can be used for realistic simulation or illustory 3D computer graphics. The result is a new form of art and science. Concepts that would once be expressed and experienced only by mathematical formulas (or linear print) can be viewed (graphics) or explored (simulations) in a medium that is much more dynamic.

The printed word is, and will continue to be, an essential part of the human conceptualizing process. The handwritten word did not replace speech and the printed word did not replace handwriting. Likewise, adding powerful electronic tools to the system will not replace print. New advances are however changing how print will be mixed into the process. One example of digitized print is the placing of all seventeen volumes of the Oxford English Dictionary onto two 4.72 inch compact optical disks (an IBM microstorage format). These 60 million words (with pictures) will soon be an information base that we can access with a microcomputer, video monitor and a modem—using telephone lines or a satellite dish. And it is predicted that within five years this will be on a single chip built into every computer or word processing program, ready to be activated by speech. Along with this, whole new vistas will open up in language and the arts. One dimension in computerized interactive literature that is just starting to become available; mixing print, visual images and group decision making. Integrating all of this with the artificial intelligence chips under development will allow interaction with a broad spectrum of language, art, and the humanities. And it allows Defense Department "Star Wars" planners to track and destroy thousands of anticipated Soviet missiles. By the next century (if we get to it) the same technology will allow us to tap into the entire sum of human experience and understanding.

Three Related Ways for Greatly Speeding Up Today's Computers

Rather than having the data wait in line, like people for a Bruce Springsteen concert, computer scientists have worked out a way that **many** (rather than one) processors can deal with a problem at once. One of these approaches is **parallel processing**. New computers, with parallel processing capabilities can be as much as ten times faster than the traditional approach. In fact it is a whole new way of building computers. The process cuts a program up and assigns a processor to work on each part—simultaneously.

Vector processing is a similar approach that is starting to be used in supercomputers. This approach takes a program apart, does the calculations together, and reassembles the program.

Multi-processing is also emerging as a different type of computer architecture. This type of new computer makes efficient use of multiple processors. Several programs can reorganize so that they can run simultaneously.

These approaches represent new ways of thinking that are breaking computer design barriers **today**.

Computer-Based Reasoning, Object/Print Recognition and Speech: New Artificial Intelligence Chips

The developing electronic technologies will have a profound effect on the three interrelated literacies that we must teach in school; print, media and computer, and the arts. New varieties of computer chips are now being specifically designed for artificial intelligence systems that analyze and alter print, images and speech. One of these chips, designed by the NCR Corporation to help robots "see," can process both print and moving pictures.

As we quadruple the number of elements on a chip every few years, we will have over one billion gates on a chip by the year 2000. And we may have as many as 10,000 chips in a single computer. This makes possible vastly improved artificial intelligence systems that act as controlling elements in a wide range of learning devices from books to images from the world's art galleries. Just as microprocessors are now found in stereo systems, automobiles, microwave oven and toys, these AI chips will be processing knowledge rather than simply information—a vast fusion of learning sytles and different media.

The Defense Department is already experimenting with such chips—allowing cruise missiles to pick out their own targets from video images. It is also possible to put this technology to work in more peaceful situations. Handled properly technology can provide a new and positive basis for the definition of education and foster a deeper understanding of our universe. Proximity Technology, Inc. (Fort Lauderdale, FL) has developed a pattern matching chip that can look for requested elements between strings of information or pictures—good for cruise missiles or a very sophisticated library/art museum search. Such a chip can fill in information from almost any set of clues—in a kind of psycholinguistic guessing game—which is very close to a definition of human thinking during the reading process.

Texas Instruments, Symbolics and Motorola are all developing artificial intelligence chips that will handle such tasks as correcting spelling, grammar and other human errors. The developing brand of AI chips simply corrects user mistakes and continues to process both print and images as requested.

"Fuzzy Thinking"

Another way of humanizing technology relates to the increasing application of the computer in ways that display what seems to be "human" capabilities. In pursuit of the salient features to be embodied in AI systems, computer scientists are investigating the relationship between artificial intelligence and "fuzzy thinking"—an idea which provides a basis for a systematic approach to approximate creative reasoning.

The concept of fuzzy thinking is founded upon the notion of a fuzzy set, which basically is seen as a continuum of possible relationships between ideas or objects. A computer that integrates this concept into its process can correctly infer from incomplete or even wrong elements of data. One practical result will be the banishment of "syntax error," the computer will decide what you really meant. Fuzzy sets underlie much of our ability to summarize, communicate and make decisions under uncertainty or partial information. In the real world which is so imprecise, fuzzy thinking plays an esential role in human cognition. This is especially true in relation to concept formation, pattern classification and logical reasoning. By building this process into computer controlled video we can give more human-like character to both (technology and humanness).

Tapping into Multiple Learning Styles

As new information technologies of the visual media and the computer begin to interact with print in a different manner new learning relationships emerge. Traditional modes of thinking merge with new learning styles to reach a broader spectrum of students. We are coming to recognize multiple levels of intelligences that include musical intelligence, spacial, linguistic, kinesthetic and intra/interpersonal intelligences along with narrow based linear thinking skills we usually emphasize in schools. Multiple modes of delivery will result in a richer variety of computer controlled print and media presentations. The result will be richer learning environments—with peers, at home and in the school.

We are beginning to restructure the manner in which we view reading, seeing, hearing, speaking and experience. Computer-based technology is starting to use symbol systems that build on "right brain" habits of thought—incorporating greater flexibility, visual imagery and intuition. Pictures and sounds combine with mathematical abstractions to form new connections and relationships and allow the user to tap into true mathematical habits of thinking which are based on creative structuring and intuitive leaps.

In considering the fact that students respond differently to various instructional strategies, it is important to recognize that not all students' personal learning styles can be addressed with a computer. Children react differently to different materials and approaches. What stimulates one student may be too complex for another. It should be expected that students will also differ in their abilities to use and assimilate the new technology. Although computers allow a variety of possibilities for educational use, there is a need to analyze who can use them with a degree of success or the potential for the new technology may diminish. A mismatch of instructional tools and learning style can hamper the learning process.

In learning to use both the new and old information technologies we will be better able to control, label, understand and manipulate experience. Traditional print technology requires the reader to connect sound-symbol relationships and organize sequentially and linearly. Computer technology involves interacting with electronic images in an emotive, creative, pattern seeking mode—allowing a fuller integration into learning areas and learning styles in the educative processes.

The Future Will Require a Knowledge of Both the Humanities and Technology

A general print, media (the visual arts) and computer-based technological literacy will be the key ingredients for coping with both human problems and the problems presented by science and technology. Instructional programs which integrate print, media (television) and computer technology are just beginning to be introduced into the classroom.

With new breeds of AI computer chips embedded into the technology future educational programs will allow for a complex mixing of telecommunications, sight, sound and print. We are just starting to move from computer information systems to knowledge systems that help us think and learn in new and exciting ways. AI chips will allow for things to happen more like both **real** and **fantasy** worlds. The possibilities opened up for learning, by the most powerful learning technology ever devised, are truly remarkable. Of course it always comes back to our disciplines—whether our role is teacher, parent, or media specialist. It is **knowing the characteristics of effective instruction** that will get us through. And knowing the principles that underlie the technology will help as we invent new roles for our machines.

Technology could very well come to emphasize human processes—and the liberal arts incorporated technology. The humanities **can** provide us with the best means of future technological inquiry. Just as "high tech" will have a powerful effect on our psychology—"high touch" will influence the future development of the technology. It is clearly beneficial to educate ourselves about both. After all, both art and science are ways of viewing reality differently.

AMPLIFYING OUR THINKING: A SYNTHESIS OF TELEVISION, ARTIFICIAL INTELLIGENCE COMPUTERS, SCIENCE, AND THE VISUAL ARTS

For the last 25 years television has proven to be the most powerful and popular communications device ever invented. Yet almost everyone is distressed by the passive quality of most programs and the failure of the medium to live up to expectations. The lack of good programming is also the most frequently mentioned negative when educational computing is discussed. At the same time there is a consensus that when television and computers are used in consort, or linked, the interactive results can be dramatic—especially for children. By adding a microcomputer to the video process the viewer can amplify the material by building on both mediums or interacting with video in new and exciting ways.

We now have inexpensive devices available that will allow the viewer to interact with the material **or** interrelate learning from both mediums standing alone. The visual arts play an important role in getting the technology across—already the graphic arts are essential to understanding everything from video science to music videos. As the present synthesis of viewing technologies proceeds we must all take some responsibility for placing these powerful educational instruments at the convenient disposal of our population.

Popularizing Science and Technology

Thanks to a tangible reality and a sustained media bath, both science and its extension, technology, are becoming popular again. Science magazines now make heavy use of visual imagery—**Omni, Science '85**, and **Discovery** are strewn about middle class households. Even the **Bakersfield Californian** imitated the large newspapers by having a weekly science section with a heavy dose of graphics. Popularizers like Carl Sagan, Stephen Jay Gould, and Isaac Asimov have become "face cards" in video journalism. "Media events" turn science and technology into a Roman Circus with sensational images that pass for "news" about artificial hearts, personal computers, and robots. Science and the visual arts permeate everything from music to medicine—to say nothing of the shopping malls and the bars (through video games) across America.

A collective visual marketing effort softens the image of science and makes technological products appear accessible. Through personalization of these inanimate objects we have injected computers so far into cultural orbit that **Time Magazine** named one as "Man of the Year." IBM has gone one step farther in their television advertisement—distorting the image of Charlie Chaplin to sell their PC to businessmen. Chaplin was, after all, one of the first to point out the dangers of both technology and business through visual images. Worse yet, some computer ads almost seem to equate the lack of a microcomputer in the home with child abuse.

How much of this media induced humanizing of technology is a commercial mirage and how much is a spiritual reaction to high tech designed to give us some assurance of control? Clearly technology and our humanness are inexorably mixed—and that mixture is popularized and exploited by the medium of television.

Video often turns an educational topic into a popular cliché. Science is popularly viewed by the media as a "search for truth" and scientists are seen as having "insatiable curiosity." Unfortunately both are very limited versions of reality. Curiosity might be better satisfied in ways other than painstaking scientific research. And major scientific breakthroughs often occur as a result of a team construction of one version of a partial truth—not simply discovering **the** truth. In fact, the most brilliant of the scientific minds do not simply search for truth; they invent it. Most of the real work of science is not the stuff of television, advertisement, news or drama.

The Delusion That Nowhere Is Somewhere (or Vice Versa)

To be influenced by television one doesn't have to use computers or join that relatively small social group that dwells in the twilight zone of the video tube. Most of us can't avoid 30 or so hours a week of passive viewing. By adding more channels and VCRs, TV today is moving in the direction of a type of narrow casting which is more tailored to personal desires. This new wider band of video illusions and reality are just merging with computers and videodiscs. In the near future, when coupled with artificial intelligence the distinction between illusion and reality will be much more difficult to judge. These new AI devices have the

Figure 16. Still image from the music video **Accidents Will Happen**, with Elvis Costello in the site "The Singing Body."

potential for creating flexible imagery adding new notes of reality and intimacy. We can tap its educational power or misuse it as intellectual novocaine for adults or as a pacifier for children. This fusion of image creating technologies will connect an endless set of human/computer controlled video variations in what amounts to a new medium—with almost hypnotic potential for knowledge building or delusion.

The Computerization of Television

Much of television production and broadcasting relies on computer-based devices in which microprocessing chips are embedded. We are just beginning to see digital television receivers with computer controlled pictures and sound systems providing greater clarity, color and possibilities for actually taking part in these visual illusions will be awe inspiring.

We could still however, be left with a visual language of blunt images (surveys show these to be most "popular") that have been defined for us with little possibility for personalized expansion. To take advantage of the new intellectual possibilities of the medium, both the producer and the viewer needs to cultivate skills in the visual arts and understand the technological possibilities for interaction. If we could merge these formally diverse areas of human understanding we would have the potential for turning the television set into a literary tool, combining electronically illustrated books (with print playing a role) and movement. We could even develop a dialogue with paintings and sculpture—a little like a personalized version of Vincent Scully's new TV program "New World Visions." New interactive video could be the catalyst for bringing literacy and microcomputers into every home that has a television set. The passive nature of current programs have definite limits. But when an informed audience can choose both the program, the printed symbols and the direction of the action—the medium takes on a creative, individualized dimension.

As both the computer-based technology and artificially intelligent programs take their place in our new Information Age, the reality of gathering, disseminating and learning may become as glamorous as the old image.

Is Television Measuring up to Its Responsibility for Enlightenment and Education?

The fact that the majority of the U.S. population uses television as the primary source of news and information points to the primacy of its role in mass communication. For all practical purposes 60 million Americans are illiterate and almost totally rely on TV for information. Even the rest of us get most of our news from TV.[1]

American television has, for the most part, become subservient to profit-making considerations and is not measuring up to its companion responsibility of serving as a means of enlightenment and education.

---

[1] Television provides us with the same news as a second class newspaper. Newspapers and TV feed on each other. For example, before putting together their evening news program, television producers carefully read the New York Times. And the "nation's newspaper," **USA Today** is little more than television news in print and static graphics.

Network discussions are usually centered around "markets," ratings and public relations.

There is growing concern about the passive acceptance of media induced "truths"—with most of our population having few critical viewing skills. As new technologies take their place the medium will become even more powerful. The viewer's taste and degree of visual literacy will determine the direction of both the personalized programming and interactive participation. Critiquing, questioning and clarifying information will become more critical to intelligent viewing.

The Fusion of Two Powerful Technologies

Combining the powerful medium of television with computers opens new vistas for education. There are, of course, a number of different possible combinations. A few recently developed educational packages combine television, computer software and printed materials. Some only require an ordinary microcomputer and television set—others require a video disc player and a cheap connecting link. No technological breakthroughs are needed—just new combinations of what's already available.

The Voyage of the Mimi, developed by Bank Street College (Columbia University) for PBS, presents a variety of scientific concepts in realistic settings and is useful for children between the ages of nine and twelve. The video segment is broadcast once a week or is available on video tape. The computer software relates to the video and contains a number of interactive activities and simulations that help explain the concepts introduced in the television portion of the program. The printed materials have science related activities and include guides for both the student and the teacher.

Solutions Unlimited and **The Voyage of the Mimi** require only a microcomputer and any television set. Interactive video requires the addition of a videodisc player and a connecting link to a microcomputer. Unlike general television broadcasts videodiscs can be almost individual in focus and specific in scope. Both NASA and the Nova program have allowed developers to adapt their videos and films for videodisc computer learning. The computer allows the student to interact with the content as the laser beam jumps from segment to segment based on the student's decision making. A student could "tour" the moon with astronauts and do scientific experiments at the speed and direction of their interest—looking at any item of particular interest. They are limited to the 54,000 possibilities on the disc, but the student is in control of that universe.[2]

A single unit microcomputer/videodisc player is just being introduced by NCR Corporation of Dayton, Ohio. NCR InteracTV is designed for educational purposes and displays videodisc images simultaneously with computer generated text and graphics, allowing the user to interact with this broad range of media. Students use a touch screen for controlling the presentation of video images, sound, text and graphics.

Artificial Intelligence and the Development of Computer-Based Instruction

Television, acting alone, lacks opportunities for viewers to interact with the visual images. Conversely, the microcomputer allows for plenty of interaction but lacks the potential for providing realistic moving images. Many children and adults now have access to both television and microcomputers, yet we are just starting to integrate the two. And no one has even started to look at the video learning implications of artificial intelligence research—which is just now bringing forward the first practical programs for connecting microcomputers and video. Computers, television, and AI programs are technologies that have complementary educational potential. The combined use of the three mediums opens up possibilities for learning and teaching that go well beyond either medium acting alone. Recent studies have found, for example, that interactive television presentations with special education students were well received because the participants could respond to the presenter.

Computational power, using artificially intelligent expert systems, is now inexpensive and practical enough to bring us intelligent interactive programming and individualized learning. Expert systems utilize knowledge drawn from human "experts," apply it to various situations and arrive at solutions. They represent the first practical applications of artificial intelligence research. At the heart of the system is a "knowledge base" in which a number of "if then" facts are stored. (For example, a child learns best with a word-image mix, the best lesson for him is one that uses both media.) The system makes inferences using a series of

[2]Video Vision Associates, Ltd., 39 East 21st Street, New York, NY 10010. (212)777-4108.

Other videodisc programs are available from Minnesota Educational Computer Consortium (MECC) 3490 Lexington Ave. N., St. Paul, MN 55113. (612)638-0600.

commands that channels information in complex loops. Through a natural language interface, the user can ask for a description of the problem of interest and receive a progress report on a particular route of viewer knowledge building—as well as the AI program's effort to help.

Expert systems allow a multidirectional interaction between the knowledge base, the problem and the user. Artificial intelligence programs can make the computer-video-viewer link more human-like in its interaction. When AI programs are added to the mix of video, computers, print and human interaction, the results are dramatic. The individual can alternate between choices based on her own experiential base and having the computer make choices based on the individual's ability and characteristics.

Artificial intelligence technology for education is just starting to become available. Expert systems are being developed that diagnose students with mathematics defiencies. The computer science department at the University of Exeter, Exeter, U.K. have devised expert systems that diagnose students with multiplication and subtraction difficulties.[3]

In the future, artificial intelligence will allow computers to more directly interact with the individual and video images. An expert AI system can "learn" about the person it's working with and respond to the individual's learning style. Whether this "mental amplifier" is going to be used intelligently or not depends on how well that application properly incorporates an understanding of learning, knowledge representation, memory and human characteristics.

Using Technology to Boost Our Thinking Capability

For the first time in the history of life on this planet a species is consciously taking the next step in its own evolution. Computer-based artificial intelligence is being used to expand human brain power by acting as an assisting tool—or by assisting learning. We are now capable of building surrogate "minds" that can handle, under our control, some of the same functions as the human mind. These programs can, with the help of video devices, conjure up all kinds of images. Some will be tapped into like a database; others will be arranged like an electronic scrapbook from a vast array of still and moving pictures. The content and direction of the exposition will be decided by the user.

[3]Attisha, M. and Yazdani, M.: **Expert Multiplication Diagnostician**, Computer Science Department, University of Exeter, Exeter EX4 4QL, United Kingdom.

The Cutting Edge of Art: Video and Film

Film and video may help to bridge the gap between art and science. Video is rapidly becoming one of the most advanced areas in art making. It is central to our understanding of esthetic and theoretical aspects of both media and art. Like good art, film and video show us how the world around us is perceived, and like science, it allows us to view the world differently. Video and film would seem to be natural allies of both art and science.

It is now possible to take an artist's work, translate it into an algorithm, and program it onto a computer. Using the same techniques we now see in advertising and in the news, it is possible to digitize paintings and allow children to play with the contents and make them move in movie-like fashion. Science, technology, and art are beginning to fuse—and by that fusion amplify each other. Videos can allow a person to enter a scene from art, literature or science and see a projected image of themselves on the screen. Their character can then change the entire sequence of directive events—almost as though the images were real. Connections can be made between a combination of diverse visual and printed images and associations. We will soon be able to weave a series of comparisons that will give substance to our curiosity—we can "interview" scientists, paintings, or primitive symbols.

Getting physical experiences form an image on a "cool" medium like today's television alone is difficult, but not impossible. When coupled with stand alone microcomputer programs and books the experience is magnified. And adding computer controlled videodisc players makes the process even more vivid and personal. The best of passive TV might give us the idea that there is an experience to be had from visual art. But using computer controlled videodisc players allow us to take part in various connecting experiences.

The computer can instantly give us a clear video image of any one of over 50,000 paintings stored on each side of a videodisc. It is possible to choose a few pictures that make up a particular line of interest. For example, one painting after another could be called up that points to a topic like political motivation in art, the influence of primitive crafts, the treatment of minorities, or the American quality of sometimes painting the women as more formidable than the men. Beyond prioritizing the line of inquiry there can be choices of rhythm and even connections to the creator's background that might help in empathy and association. All of this is possible with an Apple microcomputer, a cheap videodisc player, and an inexpensive connecting link. With more expensive equipment and/or AI programs it is possible to greatly expand the possibility of a realistic dialogue.

The Pixar division of Lucasfilm has a computer controlled machine, also called Pixar, that will transform mathematical equations into animated scenes that are surprisingly real. These images rival reality and can be used for medial diagnosis, robotic vision, oil exploration and educational simulations. An early version of Pixar was responsible for the "genesis" scene in **Star Trek II**, where a barren planet was brought to life. This and other computer based imagery devices changes the world of video/film production—from mixing sounds to rearranging scenes. Artificially intelligent programmers can make the whole thing come alive for learners.

Making realistic images for the computer controlled video screens is important to a whole range of functions beyond film and television. Machines that electronically generate and manipulate screen images are essential for people who are serious about high resolution interactive graphics; this includes scientists and artists. When images are pushed closer to human perception they can become powerful allies in teaching and understanding. The technology is used for television page turns, rotating logos, news broadcasts, rock videos and advertisements. The same machine can show a vast array of human body images, chemical reactions, atomic particles, how traffic might move in an architect's plan, the rings of saturn or the view from a robot's eye deep underground. When images and sound effects can be called up from a vast library you can get whizzing arrows that fly by at any speed and objects that don't follow the laws of physics. The dramatic possibilities for realistic educational simulations are endless.

The Future: Bringing the Experts Together

To enhance the technical possibilities of interactive computer controlled video will require a more involved collaboration between researchers in science, technology, cognitive psychology, the visual arts and those who are directly familiar with the characteristics of effective instruction—teachers.

Different combinations of hardware, software, classroom structure, curriculum materials, teacher training, and criticial viewing skills will continue to evolve as we come to further understand the characteristics of intelligent television programming and effective instruction. Video intimacy, which is already a passive illusion for a few, can become a reality for anyone interested in intellectual expansion. Rather than diminishing the play of ideas in our society, (as is the case of most current television programming) new technological extensions can allow television to amplify meaning—opening up multiple paths to learning and a larger life.

EXPANDING CRITICAL AWARENESS OF VISUAL MEDIA: GAINING ACCESS TO THE EXPLODING ELECTRONIC UNIVERSE

The computer controlled visual media, particularily television, is becoming an increasingly powerful instrumentality for the manipulation of thought. When video or film stories are controlled by computer, children can examine elements to illustrate a particular theme, project outcomes on the basis of limited information, and explore how moving images can exaggerate and stylize expression and still colonize the viewing world.

The political impact of traditional video became clear during the Kennedy-Nixon debates in 1960. And by 1966 television was affecting the war in Vietnam. On the domestic front the media began to draw public attention to both the civil rights and peace movements. The print and the visual media learned to search out individuals and groups that could conveniently symbolize issues and make ideas easier to comprehend in the 30 seconds of allotted time. Our social institution began to operate on a notion that successful movie stars had always subscribed to—the idea that the creation of an image was more important than the reality. This slick show business ethic has become incorporated into American life. Powerful visual images increasingly reflect and shape our personal and external reality. The American dream is reduced to the substance of situation comedy. Fortunately the laugh track is still there; unfortunately it's laughing at our own stupidity. As we forge new computer controlled communication links, what could be more critical than understanding the nature of these media messages?

The Good, the Bad, and the Gullible: The Making of a Political Image

The image on the evening news of Ronald Reagan playing golf with Bob Hope and visiting a retirement home for "senior citizens" (the term itself is an example of Orwelllian doublespeak) occurred the same day that the president vetoed a social security cost of living increase. The newscast reported both—but the visual images etched on the public's mind were those of a caring and emphathetic president. During the same week these masters of imagery changed the name of one of the most deadly weapons ever developed from "MX" to "Peacekeeper." When someone else (a reporter, for example) coins an image, as in the case of the "Star Wars" plan, it is seen as a coup and the government scrambles to have computer drawn animations of the "Strategic Defense Plan." The evening news shows graphic images of lasers shooting down Soviet missiles—never mind the fact that we have yet to develop the technology, and cruise missiles and bombers can go under the shield. And even if the Soviets scrapped all of their offensive weapons and did nothing technologically for a decade, a nuclear winter could result from exploding thermonuclear weapons in place. In spite of the colorful computer graphics on our TV sets what we really have is a doomsday machine insuring mutual destruction. A country could simply explode their weapons where they sit and the resulting clouds of debris would block the sunlight and propel the planet into a new ice age. Still the projected video image is one of a manageable nuclear exchange—with Soviet missiles conveniently zapped with particle weapons and lasers. And we know it's all possible—we've seen it on TV.

The symbol of standing tall, not blinking first, or imitating Gary Cooper in **High Noon** seems to be the nostalgic image many Americans prefer. And, if we are fortunate, a "photo opportunity" (which might be more accurately termed a "video opportunity") will be thrown in for good measure. A CBS news report even quotes a presidential aide as saying, "...it's the visual impressions we care about, the flags, the symbols, the balloons." Politics is just one example—much of modern life is becoming a visual illusion, a kind of show. And most of us do not have the skills of an intelligent theater critic.

The Early Stages of Mass Influence: Passive Video 1960-1985

Like microcomputers in the early eighties, television moved from the amusing novelty of the late fifties/early sixties living room to controlling (occasionally even dictating) events and the thought processes that surround them. The authentic play of ideas has been pushed aside by changes in the meaning of terms and the visual imagery of staged events and psychologically powerful moving pictures. With both children and adults spending more time with video images than doing anything other than sleeping, there is cause for concern.

Television is creating a kind of intellectual isolation for some—and protection from life too painful to endure for others. It is estimated that the average fifteen year old today has spent over 2000 hours watching motion pictures and over 15,000 hours with that other powerful instrument of visual illusion—the television set. Some of that time may have been broadly educative; **Sesame Street** can help teach children important concepts. And more adults watched the Joffrey Ballet than all ballets over the last 200 years. With its TV monitor providing us with computer information and electronic libraries of print and pictorial information, some have even suggested that the tangible physical artifacts of libraries are obsolete. But what video language are most of us learning?

The social institutions that are charged with broadly educative responsibilities need to encourage both intelligent programming and critical viewing skills. And this must be done without dismissing the value of literature and reading. The myth of the mortal book may prove just that. But as authors start to compose for electronic "books" we will have computer controlled mixtures of sound, moving pictures, three dimensional models and print. This will lead to new forms of imaginative literature, art and even science.

Connecting Visual and Print Literacy

We have a responsibility to move towards general literary skills by providing critical thinking skills that demand knowledge going beyond the 30 second news clip. Video provided world knowledge and visual experience can support the teaching of reading both print and visual imagery. As print can assist visual literacy—so too can television help us build more powerful literacy campaigns. Sixty million American adults are functionally illiterate and unable to read books, newspapers or anything else to their children. They are limited to the amputated superficiality of most newscasts—"The world is coming to an end...details at 11." If one has critical viewing skills, and a little self discipline, it is possible today to get at least the depth of our average newspaper from TV. And with new cheap microprocessor controlled subtitling devices now used by most hearing impaired people, it is possible to associate speech with the printed word. Using these relatively cheap video/print devices is just one way existing programming could aid a quarter of our population that is functionally illiterate.

The technology can even be used to help the print take on new forms and interact with computer-based video. Reading will remain the primary tool for providing the essential skills of analogue and metaphoric thinking; to say nothing of connecting us to a rich literary past. We must not forget that many other intellectually important concepts flow most readily from reading print and symbols.

The developing influence of the visual media has both positive and negative potential for affecting reading. It can be used to benefit educational efforts or to impair them. New computer-based technology may improve existing situations but bring its own set of unique problems. The same microcomputer controlled interaction of video images, print and telecommunications has the **potential** for a powerful synergism that could invigorate the process of graphically understanding important processes and learning to read print. New computer imaging techniques allow researchers to graphically share important medical information. The mapping of the polio virus is just one example. More than a million bits of information on a virus are combined in a computer to make a beautiful picture that helps researchers graphically explore the structure and come up with better vaccines.

It was Aristotle, not MTV, who developed the concept of visual music—and both had to wait for the technology to make it happen. When the full capacities of electronics are enlisted in the effort to convey information and inspiration, we will see completely new communication forms emerging. As recently as last year it was the sound produced by a musician that counted most. Now pictures and visual symbols can be even more important. The image Cyndi Lauper conjures up springs to mind before her music.

Video gives film makers possibilities for attention holding spectacular effects that are not possible with celluloid. When editing is done with computer controlled video the building of more powerful images is both easier and cheaper. Besides every other music video, two film examples are the starry effects in **Amadeus** and the spectral happenings in **Ghostbusters**. Film producers have started to transfer filmed footage to computer controlled videotape machines for greater control over their illusions. After editing the video they have technicians stitch pieces of a movie together by using another computer aided machine that avoids time consuming film splicing. Every scene is indexed in the computer memory and can be called up on a monitor for transfer to celluloid.

As the video process is further digitized there is less and less loss of picture quality. In fact, if one wants to spend the money, there are special high-revolution television cameras, recorders and tapes that are not perceptually different from celluloid. And they can be used as the primary image making method—just like film. Technological developments have made the creation of more powerful images an almost casual thing. It also makes it easy to create a lot of bad images.

Video, with both sound and color, had greater flexibility than film as far back as the 1920s. In fact, if the depression hadn't stopped television's development, the movies may have died with their mouths' shut. And we would have been intellectually poorer as a result.

Can Teachers and Parents Learn to Cope With Our Increasingly Visual Society?

We are in the beginning phase of a major communication and information revolution that those interested in learning must pay attention to. The computer controlled hardware and software is growing faster than our ability to train teachers how to apply it; and faster than parents can learn to cope. The growth of cable technology, subscription television service, VCRs, computers, interactive video, and telecommunications have also increased the impact of visual imagery. Not only have TV sets changed from a twelve channel capacity to the potential of 100 stations, but the size of the screen is getting bigger and stereo sound is being added. The sharpness and resolution of the image is also being vastly improved by microprocessors. At the same time children and adults are being targeted as video-linked consumers and saturated with visual media. Conversely neither the medium, the family, nor the school offer much in the way of visual literacy instruction.

Video Stars—Seeing Strangers as Friends

Whether it's the President or sports heros packaged by the video medium, personalized images come to be unconsciously internalized by the public and made part of our consciousness. We come to view some of these video people as friends. Whether individual or group minted images, these forces have the power to move the world in a particular direction. A carefully crafted image can result in a great deal of influence; to say nothing of profit.

Some of these elements are traditional in America; others international in scope. Both have had to wait for the technology to propel a Kennedy, a Reagan, or a Gorbachev into our consciousness on an intimate basis. If it's the "New Frontier," "Soviet Administrative Efficiency," or "Supply Side Economics," media indirectly produces an attraction and an effect—whether it's a regeneration of ideals or helping favored groups increase production. Whether or not these media induced elements are positive or negative depends on your point of view. But whatever the point of view it is essential that people have an understanding of the process.

Increasingly students and adults are coming to rely on computer controlled video databases and other technological tools. Taken together they can both decrease and amplify our creative and intuitive reasoning. If the intent is amplification then we must be able to critically read pictures and print.

Developing Visual Maturity: Interpreting Media Messages

The North American students' national curriculum has become television. This forces us to help children develop a set of visual competencies by reading about, seeing, interacting with media—and integrating this with other sensory experiences. To function intelligently in this technologically rich environment requires an ability to extrapolate meaning from imagistic impressions. The computer controlled visual curriculum will undoubtably gain greater influence—not as part of some insidious conspiracy but as a natural by-product of technolgoical developments.

Permanent change is when you can't go back to the way it was. And in spite of our occasional impulses to smash the equipment, we can't escape it. We can, however, recognize the need for developing viewing competency. Following are a few examples of specific activities that promote visual literacy:

- Move children progressively from catalogs, newspapers and magazines to television allowing them to locate features (such as packaging, color and shape) that influence what we have learned, the hard way, which is that advertisers' claims are often distortions of the reality. The image they saw was not what they got.
- Utilize home video recordings from such channels as MTV to show how metaphoric thinking (an intellectual tool, important in any area of study) can be found in the lyrics to some visual music. Ask children what can be gained or lost by accepting the values inherent

in this mixture of music, sleaze, art, stupidity and intelligence. VCR tapes can be rented cheaply from local video stores and short segments used to show how camera angle (up makes the person or object look more powerful) and symbols are used to make a statement. You can also explore how television might support less popular film types by using video tapes of movies, for example.

– Have children explore how common visualizations are created with computer-based technology for television news. Some examples here are corporate logos, page turns and graphics that show us the Soviets viewing the U.S. through the wrong end of a telescope – or Ronald Reagan taming a huge ugly bear (with big teeth) as he says that the Russian empire is the focus of evil in the world.

Using visual imagery for the child's advantage in learning requires involving parents. Most of television viewing is, after all, done at home. If the child's parents are not knowledgeable about the subject, then it is doubly difficult for teachers. Teaching students to read images in the same manner that they are taught to read print can be conveniently blended with all areas of the curriculum with little effort and a great deal of knowledge.

Looking Beyond the Imagistic Impressions of Violence on TV

Does 20,000 hours of television watching (much of which is interspersed with violence) encourage children to have fights on the playground? Programs for children contain between 20 and 25 violent acts per hour – four or five times as many as the adult shows. The average child views nearly 200,000 violent acts by the time she finishes junior high school. The influence of violent programming is inescapable, but does this issue obscure concerns at least as serious?

The hundreds of studies on the issue of TV violence prove that excessive exposure may lead children to more of an acceptance of aggressive values and causes them to develop what might best be termed a "mean world attitude." There is, however, no solid evidence that television viewing makes children more violent. There is conclusive evidence that proves that it pushes all of us in the direction of becoming more fearful of others – seeing the world as more dangerous than it really is. There is also solid evidence that powerful learning opportunities are being missed by the deadening intellectual effects of most programming.

Cutting us off from powerful intellectual tools may, in the final analysis, be the greatest danger of television viewing. The need for a full awareness of the video induced process of perceptual distortion of the world in which we live is clear. And it is just as clear that an elitist attitude towards TV will be increasingly hard to defend.

With the narrow casting of VCR tapes and new channels being added by the dozen, we must intelligently program and view our new digitized stereo television sets. As crystal clear pictures and the computer controlled possibility of interactive video come onto the scene, we can forget about pulling the plug. More powerful television products have even greater potential for enlightenment and banality. It all depends on the personal discipline and critical viewing skills of the viewer. Intelligent programming **and** intelligent viewing habits put the technology to use **for**, rather than against, people. An enabling visual skills curriculum is an important adjunct to computer awareness.

Not only does existing television have the potential for educating people visually, but also the potential to turn the medium back on learning print and thereby help both children and adults move beyond both types of disabling illiteracy. Computers can now be used to call up high-quality still photographs and motion picture segments—with the sequence of information based on student responses to the software. Neither the schools, the visual media, nor other social institutions can abdicate their responsibility for extending learning with new technology. The airwaves are a public trust for gaining access to information, knowledge and entertainment. Pacifying people with intellectually deadening electric illusions denies access to the illuminating possibilities of both print and electronic pictures.

CRITICAL THINKING SKILLS: GETTING LOST IN A TECHNOLOGICAL TRIANGLE

Middle class children today spend more time with their Apple IIs, VCRs, and music videos on their TV sets than in formal reasoning, verbally communicating, and reading put together. The same can be said of their less affluent age mates—except that they, being stuck with even more limited television and radio programming, have fewer options.

Our technological miracles are presently taking a great deal of time and giving little in return. While our students are being distracted by a tangle of electronics there is an increasing national recognition that today's crop of students is less able to critically think about the technology of their age than were their predecessors. Children today are stuck between the Sony Walkmans, video games, and MTV; understanding little about the implicit messages they carry. And they receive little help from their school teachers in critical thinking/viewing or in evaluating the technologically intensive and rapidly changing world. Since banning time thieving electronic gadgets is neither possible nor sensible, we have no alternative but to improve the programming and encourage the schools to build on the technology to teach critical thinking and viewing skills.

A Recognition of the National Need to Teach Both the Skill of Thinking and the Skill of Using the Technology Intelligently

It is both appropriate and fortunate that our students' deficits in technological and reasoning skills were recognized at about the same time. In 1984 computer-based technology and the humanities were identified by the U.S. Department of Education as the two new basics. And in 1985 critical thinking skills were added to the list. The states of California, Pennsylvania and Vermont are leaders in the trend to remedy the deterioration of thinking and reasoning skills in our student population. They will soon require mandatory instruction in critical thinking, reading, and computer literacy. This is none too soon, since several recent federally funded studies have noticed that although students at the lower end of the reading scale are reading better today than in the early 1970s; the percentage of students with higher level reading abilities (such as critical reading, for example) has slumped in recent years. Few school districts any place in the country have figured out how to help children acquire the intellectual tools needed for thinking and reading critically; or how to integrate either reasoning skills or technology into the curriculum. And no one has thought to consider how to harness those teen controlled market places of consumer technology (film, music and television) so that it can serve or at least not diminish the education process.

Our schools are making a mistake by shutting themselves off from what's important to their students; avoiding any analysis of the electronic devices (or the messages they carry) that children and young adults spend so much time with. This is added to the schools ignoring technology and over-relying on recall, memorization, and intellectually deadening workbooks. The result—which has been identified in all of the recent national reports—is the wasting of any innate ability to either think critically or deal with the new technology. Couple this with the problem of technological hinderances (primarily television) and we have a real problem incorporating thinking skills (or anything else educational or technological) into a child's life. Federally funded studies (like the **National Assessment of Educational Progress**) found that children who watch over five hours of television a day have lower reading skill levels than those who don't.

Beyond an intellectually deadening curriculum, and the failure to come to grips with either critical thinking or technological distractions, there is another factor—the quality and training of future teachers. For these are the adults that children will see as models for thinking, learning and being. It is the teacher who will play the major role in helping children come to grips with both reasoning and the new technology.

The Central Role of the Teacher in Helping Children Think and Learn About the Technologically Intensive World

A key factor in teaching critical skills for thinking and viewing our new (and not so new) electronic mediums is attracting teachers who themselves are capable of higher levels of reasoning. The teacher must be able to deal with the technology, as well as understand the thinking tools of metaphor, analogue, and deductive reasoning. If they lack this ability themselves then there is little hope in getting it across in some kind of "teacher proof" curriculum.

Why is it that the United States is having more difficulty than other countries in attracting large numbers of its best and brightest students (who have the most highly-developed reasoning ability) into teacher education? Teacher professional associations, schools of education, and governmental agencies only share in the responsibility. It is American society that must take the largest measure of blame. In countries as diverse as Japan, Cuba and Canada, teachers are in the upper third of the population in terms of academic ability (relative to other university graduates), prestige, and income. The U.S. is the only country we can identify where teachers are in the lower third in all three categories. There is little wonder that we have increasing shortages; both in terms of numbers and in terms of quality. In the final analysis, a society gets the kind of schools it is willing to provide for; and the kind of schools it deserves.

In the last four or five decades the country has had times when it most needed its best young adults as soldiers, and other times when it most needed engineers, now it is most in need of first-rate teachers. If trends continue, it is projected that by 1993 we will be falling short by 100,000 teachers a year. Something has to be done quickly, for when you have those kinds of shortages (of even warm blooded bodies) it will be increasingly difficult to address problems of quality.

What about teachers we already have in the field? Why are some of our best quitting and going into other trades and professions? In surveys of inservice teachers the most frequent reason cited was not only the low pay, over-enrolled classes, or the lack of societal support in general, but the fact that they are treated like overburdened social workers with little decision making power. Between time wasted on subprofessional tasks, like piles of paperwork and bureaucratic logistics, teachers have little time to develop and extend their own thinking-learning ability. No wonder that we have trouble attracting people with professional aspirations; people who can keep up with the literature in the field and (as teachers must) go to theatre, view current art, listen to concerts, and even read the occasional book. (Universities could help here by requiring more social science and humanities classes for those in schools of education.) Teachers, like other professionals, need to be free to create a self-renewing environment for themselves. When we have teachers who can act as professionals are expected to act (with a degree of power over their work) then, and only then, will we have stimulating classrooms where different student thinking skills are taken seriously.

Ethics and the Demystifying of Technology

Eugenics is also a good example of how science and technology can not only promise more than they can deliver, but an example of what can happen when research is divorced from ethics. Scientific investigators in the field (both accidentally and on purpose) injected their own fears into the "value free" search for truth. Eugenics pushed personal and social prejudice into public policy. The attack on this branch of science (and its technology) was led by other scientists (who warned that we simply didn't know enough to improve the human gene pool) and by Catholics who objected on moral grounds to the very principles of eugenics. But it took the Nazis to march the field into ill repute, showing what could happen when some scientific/technological principles are pushed to the end implicit in their logic. Josef Mengele was just one of many who wrote scientific articles (his were on genetics) and helped bring science into the service of the Nazi vision. In fact, it was reported that Mengele asked to be sent to the Auschwitz death camp because of the research opportunities. He even received a government research grant to support him in the setting up of an Auschwitz caricature of an academic research institute.

Although names and images may change, the past lives in both the present and the future. Science and technology are not good or bad, they are powerful, and they can be used to support social and racial prejudices. (Witness the debate over the current work of Arthur Jensen and William Shockley who claim that genetics account for the I.Q. score differences between blacks and whites.) As bioengineers use new technological tools to tinker with human qualities such as intelligence, aggressiveness, kindness and longevity, we should remember that such knowledge itself is a moral imperative.

The focused critical thinking of the anti-nuclear energy movement is one example of success in demystifying and defusing the power of a problematic technology. Our schools, whether they like it or not, are obliged to play their role in building a critical mass within our population

Figure 17. Computer Composite Image.

that can intelligently think about (and hopefully control) the allegedly incomprehensible theories and devices that scientists present us with. If science, technology and industry link up in a manner similar to the nuclear power industry of the 50's and 60's, the public will again have to foot an incredible bill for a technology that doesn't work in the end. And future bills may be more than monetary. For as Freeman Dyson, a physicist at Los Alamos Nuclear Weapons Laboratory stated, "Technology has made evil anonymous."

The Ability to Think Critically in One Area Enhances Reasoning Skills in Another

Building a patchwork quilt from elements of critical thinking, higher level creativity, questioning, science, technology, the arts, and the humanities is necessary for bringing imaginative thinking skills to our schools. Leave any element out and the power is diminished. Critical thinking and reasoning skills can be integrated into all curriculum areas; and a little critical thinking about technology can be thrown in for good measure.

Practical Examples

What are some specific techniques that teachers can use today to encourage students to think about thinking and other subjects without fundamental change in technology or methodology?

I. Visual Literature

To begin with we can help students critically view what they watch on television. Metaphors are important in the thinking process, and they can be expressed both visually and linguistically. Students can look for metaphor and simile and critically think about the values in the music videos they watch. A question that could be explored may be: What do you gain or lose when you accept the values implicit in MTV?

II. Future Studies

Examine the positive and negative effect of technology. Examine how technology pros and cons can be developed for atomic energy, computers, the automobile, etc. Discuss the need for problem solving strategies on both the societal and personal strategies levels.

III. Sociological History

Students can explore how eras in human history can be defined by the technology and related societal changes in shifting from one technology to another. What are some major defining technologies of our era?

IV. Current Events

It is also possible to take a current event on the evening news and project where it might lead. Develop several scenarios. Encourage students to identify their own point of view, and that of others.

V. Social Studies

Take an historical event, like Martin Luther posting his thesis to start the Protestant Reformation and have students develop a scenario for world history. If this hadn't happened (say he became Pope), one student pointed out, the deisel engine would have been in greater use because the internal combustion engine needed an electrical spark and electricity was opposed by the Catholic church until the 20th century.

VI. Social Studies and Language Arts

Explore the technological romanticism and the use of technology for propaganda, how can it be used to persuade, and predict. Encourage the children to become more aware of their own thinking process as they are reasoning through the problem.

VII. Creative Drama

a) Have students design a 30 or 60 second TV commercial on some technological device. Have them perform the skit for other children without props or memorization of lines.
b) Have children discuss any dreams that they have had about anything technological. Act them out in a group.

VIII. Creative Writing

Writing and thinking feed on each other. You can't have good writing without good thinking—and if we have a culture that doesn't write well, we probably have a culture that doesn't think well. Writing can heighten and refine thinking.

a) Have children take any story where they identify a technological design and write a one page story from the point of view of that object.

b) Have children apply what they have learned about thinking and writing by making abstract ideas concrete.

IX. Philosophy and Ethics

Discuss the question: How did the lack of ethical principle in the early "search for truth" by science affect the new form of poverty that came out of the Industrial Revolution? Value and listen to student responses. A more up-to-date problem might be to extrapolate from the fact that two-thirds of the money that our higher educational institutions get for research comes from the Defense Department.

X. Literature

How do the taped books (audio records of text) that can be listened to on the car stereo or the walkman, change how some people approach literature?

XI. The Humanities

a) Explore how the computer is used as a metaphor in literature.
b) Construct a sculpture out of the castoffs of our technology; old vacuum tubes, transistors, IBM cards, etc. Use paint to illustrate a concept.

Experienced teachers have access to dozens of subject matter based on critical reasoning activities. The few here are only presented to give a flavor of how critical thinking can permeate the curriculum. Teachers are encouraged to take ownership of any of these techniques that they wish to adapt for building critical thinking skills into their classroom routine. If there is a computer available, simply add it to the mix; more like clay to be sculpted than lock-step BASIC programming. Let children write, simulate situations, build microworlds, compose music, and do art with the computer technology. With or without the computer, the goal is to give students enough practice with thinking to internalize (so that it is more spontaneous) reasoning strategies that they can apply to future challenges in all subject areas, and in the real world. And daring to apply critical thinking to controversial issues is perhaps most important if we are to nurture intuitive reasoning, and assist students in using the analytic tools of scholars.

Applying Critical Thinking Skills to Technology as an Instrument of Influence

Technology and science sometimes go beyond reflecting values to helping propagate them. Subjects as diverse as substance abuse (drugs) and abortion are connected, by science, to our politics. Ideology and world view are used to justify technical distortions of the evidence. One concrete example of how the offspring of science and technology can be used to support a political position is the antiabortion movement film, **The Silent Scream**. (It is now making its grisly rounds in our high schools and colleges.) By using the technology of video fetoscopy and ultrasound it is possible to produce a TV tape of a fertilized egg. Once the tape has been cropped, edited, slowed down in one part and speeded up in another, it is possible to effectively project feelings onto the image—much like Disney projected human feelings into animals. Never mind that the 12 week fetus does not have the nervous system for a developed cerebral cortex (of the brain) to feel pain, the technology can be manipulated to make us feel that it does. Movements that physicians say are normal are characterized as "agitated" and only appear abnormal because the previous frames of "serene" floating are slowed down. Facts aside, the "scientific" image of this effective piece of technological propaganda has gained a surprising level of legitimacy.

Moral arguments and ethical positions can be obscured by imaging technology; rather than having the technology become an ally of human choice or serving as a neutral tool in building one's own moral system. Some of our gifted students pointed to the irony of having the same groups ("The Right-to-Life Committee" and "The Crusade for Life" are two examples) that want a society to save every egg also being the strongest advocates of capital punishment. (The same "pro-life" groups are the least likely to believe in societal support for women and children living in poverty.)

The point here is not to take a position in an emotional argument, but to show how controversial issues can dramatically focus critical thinking about technology. And there is the potential of developing critical thinking skills by turning a critical stoplight on science and technology's reputation as pure and objective tools in the search for truth. The potential for its alliance with anyone's point of view must be understood by those who invent, use and view it. As computers become partners in human thought we must have citizens who are capable of thinking about it intelligently.

Creative Inquiries

Opening up the flavor and texture of creative inquiry for students involves disciplined reasoning and freedom; the humanities and science, the aesthetic and the practical. It means striving for something elegant, powerful and yet fundamental.

Creativity does not just spin off from somebody's head. It depends on a certain fluency of "world knowledge" and ideas from the environment. There is no creativity in an educational vacuum. Fresh ideas must continually bounce off a person's consciousness; and computers are beginning to share that consciousness. Metaphors, analogy, and making connections where none were made before is part of the process and involves the risk of working at the edge (rather than the center) of either student or teacher competence. This means seeking intelligent criticism and viewing failure as a normal and very interesting part of the process. Imaginative thinkers rightly and wrongly grasp the nature of a problem quickly; mixing all kinds of aesthetics, attitudes, intellectual tools, (in the face of failure) and strategies to transform things into new and different patterns.

The philosophy of science and the examination of the values implicit in technology is just as important as creativity with science itself. For the creative expression to be a beneficial, benevolent contribution to the individual and society, it is frequently stated that the **source** within the person from which the creativity emanates must be determined to be both healthy and well-meaning. But what about the well-meaning creative urge that shook the earth well over forty years ago—the atom bomb? And what about those well-meaning scientific minds that are working on nuclear weapons at a furious pace today?

For every Dr. Jekyll (Salk) who uses biotechnology to modify genetic diseases and develop organisms that eat up oil spills, there may be a little of the Mr. Hyde (Mengele) who considers his views to be scientifically derived—and who is more than willing to exercise his own special form of control over the most fundamental aspects of human life—such as "sociopathic behavior." As long as scientists are encouraged to see the problems they are solving as unrelated to social policy, nuclear physicists (for example) can go about their work with little thought about the possible human consequences. With over a third of American scientists presently engaged in military work it would seem that questions concerning morality, ethics, social and personal responsibility are as important as the mechanics of science.

Thinking Critically and Critically Thinking About Technology and Education

Our technology doesn't have to simply rob us of productive time. If we learn to use it intelligently it can amplify our thinking, creativity, and learning. One step in restoring the public confidence in education is for schools to accept their responsibility for teaching both mental and technological literacy. Another is paying attetion to the programming on the electronic devices that students take so seriously. Otherwise what Bruce Springsteen just sang into my Sony Walkman will come true; students **will** "learn more from a three inch record than they ever did in school...." If schools refuse to take at least some of the things their students find important seriously then they are in danger of becoming nothing more than irrelevant day-care centers. And a society whose major institution for imparting critical thinking skills drops out of the process is more susceptible to tyranny.

Neither education nor technology radically change society's values. Rather they emphasize and fill out the ones (both conscious and unconscious) that are already there. It will remain important to teach children the mechanics of reading, writing, and computing. But if we neglect critical thinking and the skills of critically examining our technology then much will be lost in an electronic haze. The minority that is lost in television, Walkmans, video games, and MTV today will be the majority tomorrow. So we had better shape up the programming and equip our children with the critical thinking skills to deal with it.

The majority of our population already uses television as its primary source of information. And half the adults in the U.S. either can't or won't read. If we fail to enlist our technology in the effort to teach a broad range of literary skills (including critical thinking, print and visual literacy) then we can fear for both the reasoning ability of our citizens—and for our democracy. Both could get lost in a tangle of circuitry, video tubes, and microchips. What is at stake is the capacity for a resurgence in our economic, political, personal, and cultural life.

If a country is to have some semblance of being a responsible democracy, then it must have a population that is able to think critically about technology. Past scientific and technical progress has **not** always been positive or linear, rather the greatest advances have surprised us by popping out of corners. Being at least able to figure out when a scientific and technical decision affects our values and our world is important. This doesn't mean that we all have to be technologists, but rather that a significant cross-section of the population must be intelligently committed to a high quality of thinking in both the educational and technological areas. To do otherwise would insure that the worst of the status quo will prevail and both public education and mass technology will be demeaned. It is now time to decide whether or not we are going to build a first-class educational system that can help the country deal with a technologically intensive 21st century. It will not be easy. The building process will be a true test of our society's commitment to a quality of thinking and technologically assisted intellectual activity that distinguishes greatness from mediocrity.

CHAPTER 8

TEACHER EDUCATION: THEORY, ISSUES AND PRACTICE

Computer Related Learning for Teachers

COMPUTERS ARE in the process of altering both the knowledge base of instruction and the operations that teachers must apply to that knowledge base. Once teachers learn how to use the computer in the instructional process it gives them increased power over learning. There can also be a shift in the balance of classroom power if students have more computer knowledge and technological skills than the teacher. Of course it is the job of the teacher to decide the relationship of the technology to the instructional goals, but responsibility for education may be increasingly shared between teachers, students, parents and other societal groups.

Computers may have the potential of helping the schools tap the tremendous capacity the child has for understanding, learning and creating. But it is the professional attitude toward innovation on the part of the teacher that is a key factor for pervasive and permanent change in the nature of how knowledge is stored and retrieved. Computer controlled instructional technology is beginning to play a large role in providing valuable, exciting, and professionally required life-long learning experiences. One method that we have found successful in getting schools to tap into the process is to have each school identify a key teacher who either has (or is going to get) some training. They can serve as a mentor to their peers on computer-based technological training and educational computing.

There are still too few adequately conceptualized frameworks for computer applications to provide generic guiding principles or guidelines for educational computing. As with anything new, guidelines are just starting to be developed. It is teachers who must now assume responsible leadership positions for shaping the educational use of computers. The quality of courseware and software make a difference, but not as much difference as how the teacher chooses to integrate computer software into the curriculum.

The Teacher is the Key to Instructional Innovation

The speed with which the computer has been plugged into almost every aspect of American life is unprecedented in the history of technological development. The effects may be both unanticipated and unintended. In addition to helping shape change, computers may be the most important example since the printing press of a technology causing major educational innovation. But the teacher is the crucial element in determining whether or not the implementation of any new learning tool is successful. Teachers need access to information about computers to sharpen these new intellectual tools. But it isn't necessary to know a RAM from a ROM or a bit from a byte, anymore than it is necessary to be a mechanic to drive a car. (Although it might help to at least know how to change a tire.) Once you are able to steer the vehicle and use it safely, you are aware enough to use it successfully. Once teachers have some background they are the ones who should be leaders in putting demands on the publishers for more good computer software.

Everything keeps coming back to the fact that the teacher's attitude toward learning is more important than providing new technological methods or program structures. Good organizational arrangements and techniques may be successful in changing the learning environment in terms of new materials, resources, and special relationships. But new organizational arrangements are rarely successful in changing the way the teacher views the learning situation. The teacher's attitude is a critical element. To make good educational use of the new computing power requires that the teacher be flexible and open to new instructional techniques.

The Best Context for Acquiring New Learning Principles

Personal responsibility and voluntary choice, made in a setting that assists in making that choice a reality, is the best way to approach instructional change. We found that the most productive way to approach educational computing workshops was to emphasize the teacher's ability to control the computer curriculum—rejecting the control by computers.

In a communicative environment that is rich in human material, and experiential resources, the teacher can make decisions about what new ideas to accept or reject. When teachers have a hand in making the decisions and suggesting what changes are desirable, changes will take on greater credibility and authenticity than if the "experts" or authority figures initiate the type and direction of change. Taking on the feeling of ownership will increase both the likelihood, intensity, and legitimacy of change.

Computer use in the classroom may be the first major change to move from the bottom of the educational hierarchy up, rather than from the top down. Teachers were among the first to accept the new technology. But there is no freedom of choice in an intellectual vacuum; teachers need to be aware of the possibilities before being called upon to make educational decisions. But once familiar with the territory, they can experiment with new ideas and techniques and follow their own interests in using the computer as a learning tool. And in the process they can help determine the direction of educational computing.

It is particularly useful for teachers and administrators from the same school district to enroll in a workshop together—experiencing the process cooperatively. This helps give teachers not only the advice of outside experts but a support group of colleagues and administrators on a day-to-day basis.

COMPUTERS IN THE CLASSROOM: TEACHER TRAINING/STAFF DEVELOPMENT

The teacher's degree of confidence, experience, trust and support help to determine her decision to explore new attitudes toward learning and her willingness to experiment with new ideas. As more and more teachers have microcomputers at their disposal we see more teachers comfortable with them and coming up with creative applications of available programs.

A vital ingredient to successfully integrating computers into the classroom is the teacher's own frame of reference. Teachers need to feel that what they are doing is positive and significant. This requires both trust and confidence in their own ability and the child's capacity to grow and change.

Teachers spend at least 90 percent of their day with children. They have too little time for reflection or expanding relationships with other adults. It is easy to become isolated from other teachers, from the life of the school, and from the profession. Teacher inservice workshops are most successful when they supply a supportive and relaxed atmosphere. Providing teachers with opportunities to experience new computer techniques together means receiving support and feedback from professional peers. It can also positively affect the life of the school when there is good reason to work together to reach shared goals.

Simulations, games, writing on the computer, computer assisted instruction, and other open-ended activities (like creating interactive adventure stories) should be provided. Workshops afford opportunities for introducing computer languages like Logo or BASIC, using authoring systems (**SuperPilot**, for example), expert systems (Expert Ease, M.I., TK!Solver are some examples) and familiarizing teachers with the use of spreadsheets (a type of electronic ledger) and database programs that can store enormous amounts of data on various subjects. By experimenting with a wide range of courseware, student learning materials, hardware, and interactive activities teachers become more confident of their own abilities and knowledgeable about how computers can assist them in the teaching-learning process.

There are levels of computer knowledge. We define these as awareness, literacy, application and innovation. For some people **awareness** is the only necessary level. However, with the rapid influx of information and changes in educational technology it is becoming clear that teachers need to move beyond knowledge **about** computers and strive for the application level. Simply being vaguely aware of computers will not be enough to use computers successfully in the classroom or prepare students for the future.

The ambiguous term "**computer literacy**" has been greatly overused, and means different things to different people; but it definitely goes beyond simply collecting computer languages. We define it as the ability to cope comfortably and effectively with computer-related technology.

The **application level** in educational computing implies demonstrated skill in selecting and evaluating software, implementing computer-based instruction, and adapting activities and courseware to meet instructional needs. This is the level that most teachers are striving for today.

Sophisticated programming skills are required only at the highest level of computer based instructional **innovation**. Designing instructional software and creating new computer activities and materials often extends beyond the time constraints and training of the classroom teacher. Nonetheless some of our best innovations are coming from teachers today. Even some teachers who can't program themselves can design new computer courseware by using authoring systems (which allow them to do it in plain English) or hiring high school students to program for them.

Some General Guidelines for Staff Development

Inservice training needs more than someone with a computer background to help teachers. **A whole range of people and skills need to be involved.** The best facilitators are certainly not computer programmers but people with much broader backgrounds and interests. Whether on-site computing teachers are trained first or at the same time as everyone else, it's a good idea to train some local "experts" for on-site long-term teaching.

Teacher training must go beyond nuts and bolts. If it doesn't, invalid information may be imparted. Programs need to be based on research, theory and sound educational practice. Teachers must be involved in on-going, day-to-day activities. They must be able to relate and integrate professional learning to their classroom routines.

Teachers need to be able to intelligently and efficiently select and evaluate software and courseware. They need to ask themselves such questions as: Does the program improve the educative process? Will it fit into the curriculum? It is vital that educators make informed decisions to meet the needs of their students and model sound educational strategies.

Teachers need to have a knowledge of the trends and issues of educational computing.

A Needs Assessment is Needed for Some Modes of Teacher Training

A workshop leader must have some information about the characteristics and needs of the teachers participating before beginning an inservice training effort. Individual needs will vary. The elementary music teacher will have different needs from the high school mathematics teacher. Teachers will also be at different levels of computer sophistication. Some teachers will be timid beginners; others will be working at the application level, ready to explore new ways of implementing computers into their classrooms.

An informal needs assessment will enable the instructor to be sensitive to individual participants. The assessment may take the form of informal chats with participants or structured written surveys. The instructor's job is to try to prioritize and individualize the experience so that all participants benefit. Teachers should be involved in shaping the direction of the training. If there is a broad discrepancy among a group's needs and experiences, certain participants may take on the role of trainer; peer tutoring and special projects can also be arranged. The following workshop framework is meant to be adapted to fit your specific needs.

A Suggested Format for Training Sessions

Children as Teachers

Identify children and young adults in the local schools or community who have had experience with word processing, spreadsheet analysis, and some programming in Logo, Pascal, or BASIC. These students will act as tutors for the teachers. After some initial presentations by the workshop leader, teachers can work with children and teach each other (peer tutoring). Add a mixture of videotaped speakers and a pulling together by the workshop leader and you have a workshop framework.

Every effort is made to have each teacher-participant seated with a peer in front of a microcomputer with enough space to spread out papers, manuals, diskettes, and other materials.

A microverter is used so that teachers will be able to tune to the output of their own system's video monitor on one TV channel and switch to what is on the workshop leader's screen by simply changing to another channel. This allows the workshop leader to model what they will subsequently be required to do. A large monitor or projection screen will serve the same purpose.

Suggested Format for a Brief Workshop for Teachers New to Computing

Session or Hour 1

The computer itself is treated as subject matter. Educational, social, ethical, and historical/future concerns are discussed. OFF line activities that help in understanding the technology can be introduced. Specific techniques like building a computer time line, discussing how a new technology hurts and helps, or having participants collect articles about computers, etc., are some good starting points.

Session or Hour 2

In this session the participants learn about setting up the hardware and correctly running software. (Remember the computer that someone learns on is usually the one they are loyal to.) Colleagues and even students can help here.

Session or Hour 3

In this session, evaluation techniques for courseware and software are discussed and implemented. Teachers examine how to insure that the content is sound and instructionally valid before materials are purchased. Some of the software is not much better than teaching machine programs and teachers simply do not have time to develop their own. A variety of types of software programs should be made available for teachers so that they are exposed to a broad range of programs from word processing, to spreadsheets, to expert systems and to interactive children's literature.

Session 4 or Hour 4

In this session teachers develop strategies for integrating the computer into ongoing classroom routines. Staff development undertaken in isolation from day-to-day activities seldom has impact. Have teachers think about their own learning style and brainstorm how they would like to use the computer. Whenever possible let the teachers take the computer home and play with it. Most of what we have learned about language we learned by playing.

Objectives of a Full Educational Computing Class

—Introduce participants to the potential applications and uses of computers and computer-based technology.
—Provide opportunities for participants to practice basic computer operations.
—Apply research, theory, and principles of effective instruction to computer operations in application programs.

- Demonstrate knowledge of vocabulary relating to computers and hardware sufficient to adequately use and explain their use.
- Use appropriate software with sufficient competency to employ programs to advantage.
- Demonstrate facility with the equipment sufficient to add or remove peripheral devices and set up a computer for operation.
- Demonstrate an interest in computer use and gain self-confidence in using the computer.
- Discuss issues and trends related to educational computing.
- Plan, implement and evaluate teaching strategies within the context of educational computing.
- Demonstrate ability to select and evaluate educational software appropriate to level of interest.

Work Assignments for an Educational Computing Class

Weekly Session

1. Using equipment, formatting a data disk, copying files.
2. Simple interactive and menu driven software.
3. Simplified **Easy Writer** (word processing program).
4. PFS File (data entry and retrieval).
5. **Multiplan** (spreadsheet).
6. **Expert Ease** (AI Expert System).
7. Review and reaction to articles on educational computing selected from journals of participant's choice.
8. Computer uses in educational area of choice.
9. BASIC programming introduction.
10. Logo programming.
11. Selection 1*
12. Selection 2*
13. Selection 3*

*Selections: Library Literature Search
- Children's Literature
- Science and Mathematics
- Music, Art
- Television Programming
- Social Sciences
- More BASIC, **Easy Writer**, PFS: File, **Multiplan** or **Expert Ease**
- Other (by prior approval)
- Authoring Systems

Demonstrating Computer-Based Telecommunications

As part of workshops and classes we usually demonstrate some less known, but readily available, educational computing possibilities. One example is a software package that lets you tap directly into the National Weather Service's radar data bank and pull a multi-colored weather map onto the microcomputer screen. We used a 256K IBM PC, a 2,400 Baud synchronous modem, and a floppy disk from the Murray and Trettel weather software company.

When workshop participants noted that they didn't have telephone lines from their classrooms, we took a cellular mobile telephone out of the car and brought it into the educational computing class. Using a cellular model (Telentry Inc.), a Hayes software program, and an Apple II computer we quickly set up a brief three minute prearranged computer-based exchange of data with a professor in France. (It added nearly $20 to our phone bill.)

Teaching computing as a set of mechanical subskills can lead to boredom for many students. It's like teaching someone the skills of tennis but never letting them play the game. Wasting too much time on teaching tiny compartmentalized skills can kill interest. Teachers need to do real work on the computer starting from the moment they learn to turn the machine on. If we want either teachers or students to like computing, we have to give them meaningful and interesting things to do. The best use of the computer may be using it to enhance the teaching of subjects like science, reading, music, mathematics, art, social studies, writing and literature—rather than treating it as a separate subject.

Teachers need to be with and interact with other educated adults. Sharing their work and concerns with colleagues is essential to professional growth and development. Simply being with children, in classrooms, can actually prevent creativity, "excellence" and professional development.

Teachers are eager to be provided with activities to increase student involvement in the computer learning process. Our needs assessments consistently identified the desire (on the part of teachers) for meaningful, quality, student-oriented activities that can be used to create involvement in lessons. They want action-oriented projects for computer awareness and support materials for integrating computers into their day-to-day curriculum. Teachers also frequently identified the need for **hands-on** activities in educational computing.

Figure 18. Computer composite including a digitized extraction by Roy Lichtenstein.

Our inservice programs were designed collaboratively by school and university personnel. Cooperative arrangements were also worked out with local cable access channels so that we could reinforce workshops or classes with television programs and a continuing dialogue.

Computer-based technologies are infiltrating virtually every area of education at an ever accelerating rate. Implementing computers in the classroom requires more than mechanical change by the teacher. There is the extremely important element of personal change. A teacher putting the new tool to work in the classroom may experience a change that goes well beyond materials or techniques. There is the potential for change in the whole spirit of the classroom, with the teacher acting as a resource person, assisting learning in a more informal, independent, and noncoercive environment. Much of educational computing builds on both student and teacher curiosity, interest and decision making power.

Far from making the classroom more sterile and mechanical, the unique interactive properties of the computer can result in changes in both techniques and teacher attitude. Just about everyone working with children and schools is in favor of more individualization and student independence, and the computer allows us to move on both fronts. For the first time we have a technological tool that, if properly used, puts learners in control of their own learning.

Having computers in the homes may bring parents into a closer partnership with schools, a partnership generally considered essential but usually lacking. Educational software sales to the home have increased markedly. Parents often enjoy being invited into a participatory role, and availability of computers at home encourages parents to become involved in their child's formal learning. There are some problems that stand in the way of closer school/home partnerships: scarcity of computers in poorer homes, and a few parents and teachers who are unwilling or unable to become involved as educational allies.

TEACHING: THE KEY PROFESSION IN HELPING US DEAL WITH THE IMAGERY INTENSIVE FUTURE

A new set of computer controlled technological delivery systems are presenting graphic views of knowledge. With microcomputers, capable of executing one million instructions a second, linked up to graphic display screens (that have a resolution of about one million pixels) pictures are so sharp that students can build complex molecules and electronic circuits (designed with an accuracy impossible on standard video monitors). These visually intensive microworld images allow students to visualize phenomena and explore problems with greater intellectual depth than when concepts were presented only in abstract form. Ideas that were traditionally presented by mathematical formulas, print or speech, can now be dealt with more effectively through images.

For the schools to teach wisdom, as well as facts, requires teachers with a great deal of intellectual breadth and depth in not only their own discipline (the characteristics of effective instruction) but in the rapidly changing field of high technology. Teachers and students are the heart of the instructional enterprise and both need to feel a stake in the goals of an educational institution—and a sense of **ownership**. Otherwise the small daily improvements that lead to excellence just won't happen. Administrators need to ask themselves if they are living their proclaimed priorities and if they are making room for excellence to appear.

New computer-based communication devices present ideas through a medium that has been with us much longer than print—pictures. From the earliest recorded human history until the 20th century visual images served as the primary means of conveying everything from religious values, to politics, to magic. We are now going back to imagery as a prime communication tool in much of our technology—from broadcast TV to computers. The Apple Macintosh was the first widely distributed computer to use icons, and Digital Research Inc. markets a "graphics environment manager" program (**GEM Icon Interface**) that gives the IBM PC a similar capability. As far as television is concerned about 75 percent of the U.S. population already receives most of its news through these fleeting images. They also open up new possibilities in the field of robotics.

Quantum advances in imaging, computers, and communications are what led to the new submersible robotics systems that American and French researchers are using in exploring the Titanic off Newfoundland. The robots contain remote computer-controlled television still cameras and sonar mapping systems to probe the darkness under the ocean's surface. More intelligent and dextrous robots can even do ocean bottom mining.

There is a resurgence of imagery as a practical and intellectual tool. It can be put to practical use or used for understanding concepts and processes. This will not, as some claim, reduce the importance of print in a literacy intensive environment. Quite the contrary, both forms of reading (print and visual imagery) will take on even greater importance—this will be true for both the "real" and the educational world. The major change will be that print will no longer be held up as sacred—and pictures will no longer be viewed as visual Muzak. The result will be a more active and rigorous process of teaching and learning.

One positive effect of video images that our society is finally starting to absorb is the notion of career opportunities for women. And having spent thirty years getting out of the house women are unlikely to go back in all day, even if they can use computers to telecommute to their jobs. Telecommuting may be all right for emergencies, like Mondays, but people like to be with people, AND children like to be with children. Changing family structures means that schools will be with us for some time to come—if for no other reason than that the majority of children have both parents working and need a secure and stimulating place to be during the day. But if our public education institutions have to retain a status higher than sophisticated day-care centers, then they will have to take the risk of innovation. Encouraging and rewarding institutional renewal means incorporating the new technology **and** making teaching a more attractive occupation. But the goal must be more than bringing people together. Fewer than half of our seventeen years olds are adept readers—meaning that they do not have the ability to understand, summarize and explain what they read. If our public schools continue to turn out marginally illiterate students, then our democracy will suffer.

The New Electronic Imagery Requires Teachers With a High Degree of Multiple Intelligences

Interactive video combines the power and speed of the computer with the visually immediate features of television. Integrating the new electronic, visually intensive technology into the curriculum can help students learn with a personalized mix of print and visual images that can reach a broader range of learning styles. By using telecommunications technology to link a computer to a videodisc library, students can explore the great art and science museums of the world. They can examine the details of any image for as long as they wish and even summon up a print explanation. Students do not study science and art because they will all become great scientists or artists; but because both subjects provide essential fundamental skills that serve as foundations for all learning. Future relationships between disciplines are difficult to predict. The issues that physics is dealing with today were in the realm of philosophy a decade ago. A symbiosis between cultural, computer, and visual literacy may occur as a result of breakthroughs in each of these areas.

Historically everything from architecture, to clothing design, to art has used visual imagery to help people understand symbolic or abstract material. It was discovered early on that the more active the imagery the more likely it is to be remembered. From the earliest prehistoric rock painting to medieval cathedrals, visual images have played a primary role in communications.

Our technology is taking us full circle today with visual images increasingly defining our relationships to each other, the universe, and the humanities. One example of images that have a great deal of control over our youth is music video. Visual music is as undeniably exciting as it is disturbing. Along with imagery, it is shaping our children's lives far more than print. And these new icons, both good and bad, are increasingly viewed as tools of thought. Some, like the fascination of our youth with music video, are having an impact on our cultural life—glorifying a particular type of greed and sleaze. Both film and television are presenting children with the implicit belief that technology is **the** solution, rather than part of the equation.

Imagery can also function as a social conscience—witness President Reagan's visit to the cemetary where S.S. Troopers were buried at Bitburg (where such a visit could soften the image of genocide). Balancing out a visit to a concentration camp was seen by many as symbolically trivilizing the agony of the fallen victims of the S.S. Teachers must be visually literate enough to thoughtfully explore these imagery based moral dilemmas.

The television coverage of the war in Vietnam is another example of the media presenting very measured images that could not help but raise a mass social conscience. No matter how pro administration or "hawkish" their presentation, the image of Americans causing death and destruction could not be avoided. Television was in Vietnam from the beginning to the end—with the evening news visually defining the war's parameters. These images had an impact in ways we still scarcely know. (What is clear is that this imagery cannot be educationally dismissed.) During the war in Vietnam the schools avoided helping children understand either the role of television or the war. We learned nearly everything about that conflict from TV. International politics and social history were learned much like John Foggerty's song—"I know it's true 'cause I saw it on TV." At the time when we most needed schools they avoided the social issues and circled the covered wagons.

For the traditional public school system to avoid withering, they must take an active role in helping children interpret both moral dilemmas and television imagery. This isn't always easy. Only teachers who are very advanced in their own thinking can independently and adequately deal with these new literacy issues. There is no "teacher proof" drill and practice workbook to get across these important concepts so necessary for a new century. Teachers must act like any other professional and independently draw upon their own creativity, imagination and intelligence.

The Future: A Synthesis of Visual Imagery and Print

The technology for learning and communicating is developing faster than our capacity to utilize it intelligently. Many of the elementary school children we are working with today will graduate from college in the 21st century. Most of their working lives will be spent relearning how to swim in a sea of images. In this literacy intensive environment computer controlled visual systems will reason, draw conclusions, make judgements and interact through multi-sensory image rich programs.

Visually powerful technology will become increasingly important. Print will no longer be seen as the only source of information and it will, oddly enough, increase in importance as it becomes a necessary adjunct to a visually enriched curriculum. Students are already using computers to access data, make decisions, and simulate reality. To understand what they are doing, and why, children need to be both print and visually literate. Literacy, in any subject area, doesn't mean filling blanks, copying words and diagramming sentences.

Computers in the classroom change how we approach teaching and learning. For example, the traditional way of teaching reading, writing, mathematics, and computing dealt with bits and pieces—whether letters, numbers, or subroutines. It is simple to do, correct, and requires no great ability on the part of the teacher—and the testing systems that we have constructed often emphasize these skills. With the computer we really can make education meaningful for students. This should not be viewed as synonymous with being trendy or easy. Learning is more than rules. It is also more than intellectual exercise. Self-confidence and the willingness to take creative risks declines if the emphasis is on narrow mistakes.

Computers can respond to trial and error and focus on what the child is trying to communicate, rather than on component skills. And as children try to reach a wider audience they can even help them learn the rules. New computer controlled communication devices place a heavy emphasis on the whole picture using the visual senses in **inputting** and **outputting** knowledge.

Computer-based technology will force us to examine the similarities and differences between human and artificial intelligence. New microcomputer programs can be programmed with an encyclopedia knowledge of any field. Both forms of "intelligences" will be forced to make decisions before all the information (either print or visual) is in—and deal with the rapidly changing information. Turn on the computer, load some software, and you have all the rules of writing, reading, and number, you want. Teachers need to be able to operate as decision-making professionals for our students to benefit from the information explosion and the availability of new technologies for delivering education. New inexpensive microcomputer software containing AI expert systems are coming onto the market. They can take care of all of the component rules of most subjects, but they can't read a poem, or think through a story like a child.

Intuitive reasoning techniques (whether scientific or artistic) are coming to be recognized as crucial elements in the processing and applying of large amounts of unfamiliar pictorial and print information. And computers have yet to reach a stage where they can deal with the most human of elements. The visual arts and science disciplines are coming together as the realization that science is an evolving process, rather than a set of component skills or absolutes. Art has something to offer science in its effort to view reality differently. Both art and science require a flexibility of visual models. Relatively inexpensive microcomputer technology makes as much use of visual imagery as it does print. And this same technology relies less and less on rules and component skills and more and more on the creative imagination. The worst mistake we can make in this new technologically intensive era is to give the child drill sheets and dittos and make them memorize the component elements of a subject.

Attracting Teachers Who Can Engage Students in a More Active Process of Thinking and Learning

Our knowledge of the instructional universe and the things in it changes and expands at extraordinary speeds. A wide range of electronically based communication skills will be required of students as we experience an explosion of image based creative thought. Hopefully we can at least control the direction of the blast as students move through an increasingly intensive environment. Computer controlled technology can build programs based on the fact that many concepts can be learned best through a mix of images and print. Technology can be used to access, convey and tailor information in a manner and context that is most useable for the individual learner—and provide us with new insights into human learning. But to make it work for children we need a drive to bring our best and brightest college students into teaching.

The public dissatisfaction with the entire public education system runs wide and deep. But if the public schools become a type of adolescent day care center for those who cannot afford private education then both haves (the majority of whom are white) and have nots (primarily non-whites) will suffer because the public schools serve the important societal function of homogenizing cultures. Just when educational reforms are being called for—from the federal to the state level—one of the worst teacher shortages in decades is threatening any hope for reform. If technology can help us in raising teacher productivity and addressing a multitude of instructional concerns, than it is sorely needed. But can we attract the kind of teachers we need to work systematically at improving schools? Our dire need today is for the best of our youth to dedicate themselves to becoming teachers. The quality of our teachers means everything to the future of the country. With no reduction in class size, we will need to recruit more than a million new teachers over the next five years. This is more people than we need to induct into the armed forces during the same time period.

The last time such a shortage occurred, during the postwar baby boom, many states decided to save money by simply lowering their standards for teachers—contributing to a decline in school quality. This time, fortunately, the combination of national concern about the quality of schools and the teacher shortage will drive salaries up in the effort to attract and retain the best people. Not only are we approaching a severe shortage, but a series of critical reports have pointed to a real need to revitalize teaching and learning. We will, however, never attract the best people by treating them like lower level bureaucrats who spend most of their time on sub-professional tasks. The new bureaucratization of teaching practice is a far cry from **excellence.** Our brightest college students expect to choose careers where they can have a major role in setting policy and making professional decisions about what they do and how they do it. They sense, rightly, that a professional person is trusted to operate independently, is well compensated, and makes important decisions. If technology can encourage improvements then it should be embraced, and if education is as important for the future as everyone says it is, then we have to change the image of teaching itself—making it a more attractive choice. So structural changes must accompany a major campaign to attract a million plus teachers with ability and commitments.

THE FUTURE OF TEACHER EDUCATION: PAYING THE PRICE FOR NEGLECTING IMAGINATION AND SCHOLARSHIP

Schools of education have a mission that transcends the narrow concept of pedagogy that is the current focus. To become academically respectable within a university setting, teacher education—if it is to remain a viable field—must go on to the creation of knowledge. This means enhancing both scholarly activity and creative ferment in the imagination of the faculty involved in training perspective teachers. They must go beyond the "terminal degree" (PhD) to rigorous life-long learning and active participation in the world of ideas. This kind of faculty development requires an extended effort that pulls teacher educators away from the comfort of their parochial environment to come into extended contact with the best and most advanced thinking in their field.

Schools of education realize that faculty development is only the first step in refurbishing their intransigent image. Frequently they react to criticism about the quality and mission of teacher education with public relations efforts to appear academically rigorous. Testing perspective teachers is often instituted to tighten up the image. Yet cramming for tests (at all school levels) is mentioned in the research as a device that replaces real intellectual involvement. There is almost an obsession with image—with substance fading into the educational school background. Image, it seems, is a powerful reality that often translates into requiring intellectually limited tests and the setting up of more treadmills of busywork (that focus on a narrow range of thinking-learning styles). Since many of our most intellectually qualified students refuse to subject themselves to much of this deadening nonsense, we shut the field off from some of our ablest potential recruits (to say nothing of our minority students). The cleverest college students simply refuse to consider a profession that does not encourage independence and iniative. We are losing the possibility of attracting some of the most academically qualified students to the field. At the same time we are neglecting the art of stirring the intellectual, emotional, or aesthetic appreciation (of the world) of the students we do have. Having states and local school boards require children to spend more hours on instructional tasks will not improve the educative process unless we have more and better instructors.

Neither the analytic tools of scholarship nor the nurturing of the creative imagination is given much credence in teacher education today. The result is a diminishing of the human capacity for imagination and thinking—for both perspective teachers and their future students. Little wonder that some states are starting to look to university arts and sciences faculty to train teachers—cutting teacher educators completely out of the process. In many of our largest cities—from Los Angeles, to Houston, to New York City, school districts are beginning to bypass schools of education by hiring college graduates who have no education credits. New Jersey is another example. It now allows anyone with a bachelor's degree to teach after passing some basic skills tests and agreeing to take part in workshops during the first year of teaching.

Figure 19. Digitized picture from **Alice in Wonderland.**

By diminishing the quality of the ideas that students in teacher training courses must grapple with, we put the field in jeopardy and potholes in the road of educating our students. A society chooses its future through the education of its children. Unless teachers are trained to respect the creative life of the mind—and believe in learning for its own sake—schools of education will have difficulty reasserting their influence in the preparation of new teachers. Avoiding tough controversial material results in a retreat from higher standards and a watering down of the curriculum.

Do Ed Schools Confuse Being Receptive to Change With Being Trendy?

Every few years we hear from authoritative notices that something is about to redefine the educative process. Each wave of excitement about some new educational concept or device is followed by a disappointment that we have not discovered a mythical cure-all for teaching and learning. Of course the fact that few of these innovations reach very far into the schools is not considered. Even with the rush for schools to acquire computers we still only have a ratio of one for every sixty children. Writing that innovation off now would be like writing off using books to teach reading because we only have one book to share between two classes—and, as a consequence, we find out that books aren't very effective learning tools. Educational computing, like any experiment, will find the answers of its usefulness at the end rather than at the beginning of the process. The real concern here is with **how** we are approaching this key element of change in a period of serious identity crisis for teacher education.

The development of silicon-based microprocessing chips has resulted in a major technological innovation—the microcomputer. The computer, as we know it today, may or may not exist in schools of the future. But certainly it (or a similar device) will control much of our future educational technology. And, as education seeks to adjust to and utilize this new technology, strategic planning **is** needed to build educational computing into the teacher training process. As can be expected, the scope and pace of technological development outstrips our ability to understand and utilize it.

Although subjects like computer programming are comfortable for the organized teacher's college type of mentality, we have little evidence that the skills involved have much to do with either the future or with teaching students how to learn and reason with greater intellectual depth. Consequently, learning programming languages will probably have a relatively small role to play in future schools. Authoring systems will allow the computer to do the programming after it's given its instructions in plain English—making language skills more important than computer skills. As we learn to use artificial intelligence programs, word processors, electronic spreadsheets, telecommunications, and computer controlled video-voice-print technology we will need all the human skills we can get. Computers may be the most powerful learning technology ever invented. But their near and long term educational repercussions are difficult to predict. Certainly the incorporation of computers into teacher training will not, by itself, invigorate the process.

Structuring Learning for Multiple Thinking Skills

Although its focus has been too narrowly defined, the computer is a tool that educators can help align more closely with the humanities. Children can use the computer to understand concrete processes—manipulating both objects and knowledge in a concrete personalized manner. The computer is simply a delivery vehicle and the imaginative quality of goods being delivered remains unmapped.

The debate over computer use in schools is over. Microcomputers are here to stay and teacher educators have to make the best of them. The question is how to use them for enhancing, rather than diminishing, the human capacity for intelligent creativity. The thinking skills that help students reason divergently or that stir aesthetic appreciation of the world cannot be divorced from educational technology nor taught as enrichment—**nor** as subject matter. Rather the more difficult route of teaching all subjects in a stimulating manner (of some intellectual depth) is necessary for any transfer of that thinking to other areas.

The Imaginative Analytical Tools of Scholarly Thinking Must Permeate the Entire Curriculum

Teachers and teacher educators have time-tested techniques that work here—creative drama, movement, creative writing, selected literary experiences, the scientific method, deductive inquiry, group investigation, fantasy, the exploration of dreams, language experience stories and simulation are just a few examples. Basic skills in reading, writing and science/mathematics **can** be improved along with aesthetic feeling and intuition. Simplifying textbooks and denuding the curriculum of intellectual challenge is not the best route for reaching the child's mind. And drilling students to come up with the right answer does not improve knowledge, understanding, independence, logic and the ability to think critically. Intellectual tools to think metaphorically, understanding the use of analogue, and an understanding of the scientific method, can be built into every subject so that we can teach thinking skills effectively. And doing this with teacher trainees today will impact the schools of tomorrow.

Education must have many dimensions. When students come to school, they have an insatiable curiosity about the world. Teacher educators can participate (both with and through their students) in building a rich school environment that amplifies that inquisitive intellectual curiosity about that world. If we constrict the educational experience of the perspective teacher by a combination of narrow world view—and a constricted type of educational fundamentalism—then we can expect little in the way of ethical development or higher level thinkers—diminishing naturally searching and open minds.

The Role of Teacher Education Programs in the Future

University departments and schools of teacher education are in some danger of simply fading away—slowly relinquishing their hold over programs required for entry into the teaching profession. A number of the national reports on mediocrity in education place the blame on schools of education and recommend their elimination as the formal unit that decides entry into teaching. Several of these reports suggest that arts and sciences graduates be certified to teach without professional education.

The field of education must demonstrate that it has a body of knowledge (of some intellectual depth) **and** a faculty capable of contributions to the advancement of that knowledge. If both are not on a par with other disciplines we neither attract the number of highly capable students we need to meet the expanding teacher shortage nor continue to exist as the entry passage into teaching.

Even research that doesn't advance the frontiers of knowledge benefits teacher education indirectly by stimulating faculty, students, and the curriculum. If teacher educators are to play a major role in the future of the profession they must be capable of both creating new knowledge and using that knowledge in the preparation of new teachers.

All is not gloom and doom in teacher education. There are established pockets of excellent scholarship. Many teacher education tools **are** extending the limits of knowledge in the field. Inquiry, research practices and the collaborative innovation of curriculum structures **is** occurring. The heightened academic and public interest (even though much of it is negative) **can** provide both the impetus and the resources for both faculty development and the attraction of new scholars. To do this requires a rigorous return to insisting that professors in the field be competent enough to work toward adding to the body of knowledge in the area. Otherwise more and more teacher training will continue to slide away from schools of education to on-the-job training in school districts.

To invigorate their own teaching and move the profession in a viable and exciting new direction teacher educators would seem to have little alternative to maintaining their interest in the world of ideas and renewing their publication and research efforts.

CHAPTER 9

MICROCOMPUTER-BASED TELECOMMUNICATIONS: TAPPING INTO ELECTRONIC NETWORKS

WHEN YOU THINK about the educational use of computers you have to think about the telecommunication possibilities. In fact, electronic networks are one of the more dynamic possibilities in microcomputing today. We already have an Electronic University (headquartered in San Francisco) that is open 24 hours a day. Students are spread across the country and anyone with a microcomputer and a modem can enroll. There are links to 25 university computers so that students in the network can get accredited degrees. Simpler products, dropping prices, and a broader range of educational materials to choose from have increased the instructional benefits. Using computers to communicate over long distances with other people, computers, and databases can cause exciting educational things to happen. There are all kinds of ways to do this—combining computers, telephones, (both with and without cords), satellites, lightwaves, broadcast and cable technology. These recent developments in the march of computer accessed telecommunications are important for educators to understand. Schools now have the possibility of using computer-based interactive text, graphics, and simulation. Such things as computer programs and joint writing efforts can now be exchanged between schools that are great distances apart. These learning webs can bypass knowledge monopolies with an open exchange of information.

It is even possible to bypass some of the hardware, like modems (those small inexpensive telecommunications devices attached to the computer). Telephone lines can also be replaced with various kinds of microwave broadcast signals that allow computers to communicate with one another.

Using a modem (and a telephone) is still the most common way to telecommunicate with microcomputers. By buying a cheap communication software program (being sure that you have a modem attached to your school microcomputer) you can use any telephone line. Modems and communications software (that do the work of making the connections) are getting better and easier to use. Even inexpensive modems do a good job of translating signals to travel through telephone lines. Most now offer menu selections and take care of translating your instructions onto the software that actually moves information around and accesses networks, information databases (like CompuServe), and electronic mail services (such as MCI Mail).

Simply make the connections to a telephone (or use a wireless portable modular phone), then insert the software into the disk drive, and you are ready to go. Millions of children are already involved with microcomputer telecommunication at home—so you probably have a child in your class who can help the process get started.

The educational benefits of microcomputer telecommunications are growing along with ease of use, remote access, full text (print and visuals), unattended operation, security, and faster transmission speeds. Whether it's browsing through an on-line database library, transmitting messages, or supporting distant users by remote control, microcomputer networking adds an exciting new dimension to both educational computing and the budget for telephone charges.

Examples of What Children Are Doing With Microcomputer Telecommunications Today

Chatting and Electronic Mail. Chatting back and forth to communicate is simply using a computer much like a telephone call, except that children develop writing skills by typing the message on a keyboard—and the print appears on a distant computer screen.

Electronic mail is like the standard U.S. Post Office mail, except that the letter moves at the speed of light to the addressee's computer. It is even possible to provide instant electronic communications to users of otherwise incompatible microcomputers, terminals, word processors, and main frame computers. The mail can be accessed instantaneously, or "picked up" (viewed) at the receiver's convenience, like regular mail. The "letter" can be sent through a third party computer (like MCI Mail, Western Union, Easy Link, and Federal Express Zapmail). It is even possible to send a letter from Los Angeles to New York electronically, have the hard copy printed, and deliver it like regular mail.

Electronic bulletin boards. A cross between public electronic mail and a newspaper, electronic bulletin boards can be accessed by anyone with a modem-equipped microcomputer and telephone. (In some cases you need an access code.) And practically anyone can start one.

Documents. Documents can be exchanged by microcomputer. Students in different locations can write a story together or jointly interact with a literary concept.

Conferences. This is where individual groups in diverse locations can take part in two way communication. Conferencing is particularly effective with the new computer-based video devices that allow participants to see one another on a split screen. Inexpensive digital compressors can be attached to a microcomputer, allowing color television pictures to be transmitted computer to computer, on regular telephone lines.

Libary. This contains both documents and software. Students can upload or download software or documents from them. Smart publishers are starting to use such libraries as distribution outlets. Computer programs are now being used that read printed text out loud to students. It is especially useful for the visually impaired or young child who enjoys being read to. The computer can read the text looking for specific concepts and stop to orally read particular passages. With computers like the Kurzweil Reader you simply place the book on top and the computer reads it out loud.

A few libraries are also starting to include expert systems, a computer program containing the elements of an expert's decision making behavior. Some libraries will soon be able to construct artificially intelligent expert systems that allow microcomputer users to interact with simulations of notable writers and literary experts.

Technological developments in computing, video, and telecommunications have the potential of dramatically transforming educational activities. But at least one of the possibilities, the electronic bulletin board, is not being neglected. The use of this microcomputer accessed telecommunications medium is growing by leaps and bounds.

Microcomputer Accessed Electronic Bulletin Boards: In Place and Functioning Today

A microcomputer, telephone line, modem and software program allows students and teachers to communicate with others in diverse locations through a vast and varied network of over 3,000 electronic bulletin boards. This form of mass communication is less regulated, cheaper, and more accessible than other mediums. The electronic medium provides rapid international communication among large numbers of people in diverse locations.

There are dozens of commercial computer accessed bulletin boards. The Source, CompuServe, SpecialNet, TechCentral, DeafNet, and the Dow Jones News/Retrieval System are just a few examples. These are like electronic magazines that can be used by schools, businesses and government agencies. **AECT** is just one example of professional organizations that uses its "TechNet" computer-based electronic network to communicate with members. Large commercial databases, like CompuServe have as many as 200,000 subscribers and 100 bulletin boards to choose from. But anyone with a computer, telephone, and a $50 software program can start an electronic messaging system. This gives these microcomputer accessed bulletin boards the lowest entry cost of any mass communication medium.

Millions of people are now exchanging information using their microcomputers and telephones—making this medium an important information resource. Most of the material on electronic bulletin boards involves the exchange of information—from the best educational computer software, to research in special education. On the dark (or at least dim) side there are bulletin boards with stolen telephone credit card numbers, "Micro-Smut," "On-Line Wine," Herbal Recipes, and "Dial-Your-Match" dating service. This powerful new mode of communciation enables publication (educational or otherwise) without a printing press.

Computer accessed bulletin boards are nearly untouched by existing law. Is the computer bulletin board analogous to a newspaper, a supermarket bulletin board, a telephone company, or a newspaper? The answer to this question will probably determine how operator liability will be considered in the future. Attempts to restrict such communication raise serious First Amendment (to the Constitution) problems. Fortunately laws are now on the books to prosecute computer crime, so new laws to restrict the freedom of expression would seem unnecessary. And besides, laws governing the nature of the material on electronic bulletin boards would not only clash with freedom of speech and press but be difficult to enforce.

Many states have included lessons on the ethical use of computers in their educational computing curriculum—with computer fraud being viewed as serious as other types of crime. But there is a deeper social concern than the simple crime of using stolen credit card numbers. Like any technology there is a potential for good **and** bad. A group of American neo-Nazis (called the Aryan Nations) and the "Computers for Christ" system communicate regularly by computer bulletin boards. Computer pirates have burnt software publishers downloading their programs onto electronic bulletin boards where they are free for the taking. Some hackers also enjoy tapping into private networks—whether it's a news service, credit rating firms (like TRW), or the Defense Department. They get the passwords and numbers that make this possible off electronic bulletin boards.

Many students use these computer-based telecommunication systems at home to discuss rock music, new computer equipment, and to play simulation games. Some have taken to placing notes next to their comments that communicate shades of meaning—like "hee haw" or "kisses." Whether children in school, or teenagers and adults at home, the range of interests and approaches to this very accessible medium are as diverse as the users. And like magazines, they can be good, bad, or indifferent; but they are being used **now**. Of course, years will pass before we have solid answers from the research about the effect of computer-based telecommunications on learning, because the hardware, software, and databases keep changing before the research gets off the ground.

Some Examples of Data Networks Now in Operation

Nationally, public broadcasting stations (PBS) are starting to exchange information via computers. Interactive video, electronic text, and teleconferencing are part of a year long demonstration by PBS affiliate KUON-TV (The University of Nebraska-Lincoln). In a related venture an on-line database service (DIALCOM) is managing electronic bulletin boards and electronic mail service involving more than 50 public broadcasting organizations. In yet another telecommunications venture, Globenet and Satellite Broadcast Network are joining forces to offer direct computer broadcasts from satellites to microcomputers.

All kinds of routes for computer controlled telecommunications are being explored. Equatorial Communications Corporation has entered an alliance with G.E. Information Services, and Bonneville Telecommunications for broadcasting computer-based information from satellites to earth stations—which in turn, send them out to microcomputer users on FM subcarriers. Even cable TV is getting in the act by launching a computer downloading service that is delivered by cable TV. (Discovery Broadcasting initiated the service in the Los Angeles area.)

Whether using direct (to microcomputer) broadcast, microwave and lightware transmission, fiber optic cable, telephone lines, satellites to earth stations, or some exotic mix of several of these carriers, microcomputer users can easily access all kinds of databases and electronic pipelines.

Moving Toward Future Computer-Interactive Video Courseware and Software Databases

In the fall of 1985 Maryland Instructional Television (a division of the state department of education) opened a database network that can be accessed by school microcomputers. This PBS affiliate broadcasts new software packages, their updates, general information, and custom data packages to schools. Schools are allowed to tap directly into a range of software, courseware, and interactive video **without** using any telephone links. Classroom microcomputers can communicate with a central school computer that contains current information and computer-based instructional material on a broad range of topics—from science to the language arts. The central computer reviews updated information and new computer courseware via satellite from an even larger mainframe computer at the Maryland Center for Public Broadcasting. The Maryland Department of Education sees this computer-based telecommunication utility as a cost effective means of supplying educational software to local schools. There are no modems and no phone bills on this "educational utility system," airwave frequencies link computers. Students use of individual programs are metered (by computer) and publishers review royalities based on how often their software is used. Maryland Public Television uses a broadcast subcarrier for sending information to over 500,000 students simultaneously. Public Digital services are also starting to be offered by telephone companies. Pacific Bell, for example, is offering bulk data transfers (between computers), slow scan video teleconferencing, digitized picture transmission and electronic mail. New communications software programs allow microcomputers to simultaneously handle up to 15 channels over a single dial-up telephone line.

Dialing into Databases—Here Today, More Tomorrow

At the moment we have three types of commonly used microcomputer based telecommunication networks. The first is a type of microcomputer network like CompuServe or The Source. The second is a videotex system like Viewtron or Gateway. And the third is the type of teletext system offered by CBS and NBC.

Teachers and students can use the communication power of distant mini or mainframe computers by connecting a modem to the communications card in their microcomputer and inserting a software program into the disk drive. Schools can also make use of telecommunication possibilities by tapping their microcomputers into existing data networks. (Remember some of these services do require a subscription fee and password.) If they want to go further they can create local area networks of their own or download electronic text via broadcast teletext or videotex for storage in a student's microcomputer. School districts can build computer-based teletext services with local television stations, cable channel, or a district wide closed-circuit TV system. It is also possible to create a videotext service (that classroom microcomputers can tap) on a district mainframe, mini-computer, or powerful microcomputer.

Networking microcomputers for the purpose of exchanging information holds great promise for promoting critical thinking, communication skills and providing access to the world of ideas. Computers are making it possible for students to interact (communicate) with other students, video discs, films, books, databases, and other educational media. Students are already using such systems to explore a variety of topics, construct webs (a type of visual outline) and write drafts of stories with schools thousands of miles away. It is time for educators to take purposeful steps to take advantage of this new set of flexible microcomputer tools that can be used for learning at a distance—tapping into centralized libraries (or museums) and a myriad of other communication possibilities. These **are** major educational implications for the computer telecommunicating possibilities in place today. And the computer controlled networking tools on the technological horizon will enhance the instructional process even more dramatically. Computers will move from tools to partners in assisting human thought.

Resources

Information Utilities and Databases

Most information utilities are most efficiently accessed through special telephone services, such as Tymnet and Telenet. Each service has different fee schedules, which are explained as part of the sign-up procedures for the information utilities it services.

The Source

The Source
1616 Anderson Road
McLean, VA 22102

The Source includes databases and services over a broad scope of topics, including electronic mail, bulletin boards, newspapers, public domain software, shopping, and computer conferencing.

CompuServe

H&R Block Company
5000 Arlington Centre Boulevard
P.O. Box 20212
Columbus, Ohio 43220

CompuServe's services include electronic mail, a national bulletin board system, a CB simulator (which allows the user to have multiple conversations with other users in real time), news and information, business information and services (Dow Jones, etc.), personal computing services and information, electronic banking and shopping, computer conferencing, electronic games, and on-line *World Book Encyclopedia* references.

ERIC

Available on DIALOG, ORBIT, and BRS

This contains the information compiled by the Educational Resources Information Center. The indexes are updated monthly.

DIALOG

DIALOG Information Services Inc.
Marketing Department
3460 Hillview Avenue
Palo Alto, CA 94304
(800)982-5838 (California)
(800)227-1927 (other states and Canada)

DIALOG contains over 200 databases. *Books in Print, International Software Directory, Microcomputer Index, Newsearch*, and *Book Review Index*, are only some of the listings which encompass business, social sciences, chemistry, medicine, technology, engineering, law, government, and education.

BRS

Bibliographic Retrieval Services
1200 Route 7
Latham, NY 12110
(800)833-4707

BRS provides on-line searches of professional databases. It includes ERIC, Exceptional Child Education Resources, Bilingual Education Bibliographic Abstracts, National Information Sources on the Handicapped, National Rehabilitation Information Center, Psych INFO, *Academic American Encyclopedia*, ABI/INFORM, MEDLINE, and Compendex, as well as a variety of other professional databases.

ORBIT

Orbit Information Retrieval System
SDC Search Service
2500 Colorado Avenue
Santa Monica, CA 90406
(800)352-6689 (California)
(800)421-7229 (other states and Canada)

ORBIT includes over 80 databases. Accountants, APIT, COLD, MONITOR (Christian Science Monitor index), and SPORT are exclusive to ORBIT.

The Information Bank

New York Times Information Service
1719A Route 10
Parsippany, NJ 07054
(201)539-5850

One of seven databases available from the New York Times, The Information Bank includes abstracts from all New York Times articles since 1974, plus abstracts from twelve other newspapers and over forty magazines.

Dow Jones News/Retrieval Service

Dow Jones News/Retrieval Service
P.O. Box 300

Princeton, NJ 08540
(609)452-1511 (New Jersey)
(800)257-5114 (other states and Canada)

This database includes the Dow Jones News, World Report from the United Press International, and Wall Street Journal Highlights Online.

Educational Bulletin Board Systems

There are thousands of electronic bulletin boards that range from children's messages to teenlines to financial reports. Included is a sampling of some bulletin board services geared toward educators.

SpecialNet

SpecialNet
National Association of State Directors of Special Education
1201 16th Street NW
Suite 404E
Washington, DC 20036
(202)822-7933

SpecialNet contains over 25 topical bulletin boards including: ASSESSMENT, ASSISTIVE DEVICE, CEC News, CHAIN, Early Childhood, EDUTECH, EXCHANGE, Gifted, Multihandicapped, OPINION, CSPD, PRACTICES, RFP and SLATE.

Free Educational Bulletin Boards

Educational Technology PMS (People's Message Service)

San Diego State University
Department of Educational Technology
(619)265-3428

The purpose of this free bulletin board is to allow educators to communicate about microcomputer telecommunications technology.

Handicapped Educational Exchange (HEX)

c/o Richard Barth
11523 Charlton Drive
Silver Spring, MD 20902
(301)593-7033

Living Bulletin Board System for Educators

Computer Using Educators and the Far West Regional Educational Laboratory
(415)565-3037

Notre Dame Bulletin Board System "The Leprechaun"

(219)239-5875

MOVING TOWARD COMPUTER CONTROLLED GLOBAL COMMUNICATION NETWORKS: HOW TELEVISION IS FORGING NEW THINKING PATTERNS

Computers and video technology are inexorably linked; you need one to view the other. By analyzing the patterns of the older technology (television) we may be able to anticipate future human-computer-video interactions. In fact, television could serve as a metaphor for future computer controlled technology—human communication.

We have now reached a stage where events outside of ourselves seem unreal if they do not appear on television. We are even coming to depend on it for perceiving the difference between what's real and unreal. American TV may be inconvenient, intrusive, and subtly harmful, but it is becoming a central condition of being over much of the globe. Video is now beamed 22,000 miles to a satellite in space and beamed down to any place on the planet at the speed of light. Unfortunately imagination and intelligence are often missing from the programming it carries—and the language that TV uses is based on a very limited vocabulary, shattered sentences, and simplistic thinking levels. Although this may be helpful to those just trying to master simple language patterns, TV English is not very helpful for those who want to move beyond a fourth grade vocabulary. And it is downright harmful for those trying to move to higher levels of thinking.

Recent communications/computer alliances set forth a global strategy of using new technological combinations to bring visually based ideas and information to a world-wide audience. (The recent IBM, CBS, MCI alliance is just one example.) These multinational computer-communication combinations intend to serve up video as well as data. Unfortunately the TV packages that are a main part of the mix (for the mass audience) do not point the way toward literacy, nor cultivate the kinds of language and thinking skills that children will need in a literacy thought intensive future environment. In fact, the miracles of our new technology may contribute to the erosion of literacy and language patterns on an unprecedented world-wide basis. Yet television has great holding power—and we all seem destined to spend more time watching the video tube than reading, writing and speaking put together.

In the United States, more time is now spent on watching television than doing anything other than sleeping. The majority of children and adults (in the U.S. and other industrialized countries) has come to depend on TV for intellectual perception as much as a minority has come to depend on junk food for nutritional sustenance. And, whether we like it or not, it's likely to remain that way. The problem is to maintain intellectual standards while using technology itself to turn around a technologically induced diminishing of literacy and human visual perception. The difficulty is compounded when we are forced to handle the powerful synergism that will be progressively released as video merges with other technologies. As television itself undergoes radical change we could find that it is a fine line indeed that separates the meaningless from the meaningful.

How Current Broadcast Television Affects Children's Language Skills

Television points up the unsolved societal/educational problems of reconciling technological innovation, political democracy, economic monopolies, foreign competition, and a panorama of unmet educational needs. Heavy viewing seems to bring children evaluated as having excellent English language skills (writing, reading and speaking) closer—in terms of test scores—to students with lower language skills. Our informal survey suggests that TV does this by lowering the scores of its brightest viewers and upping the scores of the lowest. American television typically uses a lowest common denominator formula to bring a mass audience a serialized story that focuses on the obvious—avoiding any linguistic or intellectual complexity. Hopefully the refusal of many states to go along with watered down lowest common denominator textbooks may be extended by the public broadcast television.

In our survey of the language building potential of American television we found that prime time programming was limited to about 4000 different words—with very little use of metaphor or other concepts requiring higher levels of thinking. For programming to aid in language development would require a doubling of that number; the average high school or college class makes use of over 10,000 words. Lack of intellectual complexity and sentence length is another problem. Television scriptwriters tend to stick to obvious concepts and use sentences of about five words in length. Sentences in nonfiction books average over twenty—and the worst book has to make some use of metaphoric thinking.

What students read and what they see and listen to on television affects their writing style and their thinking. When students watch television, to the exclusion of books, the result is fewer words and simpler sentences in their own writing. Since television programs contain primarily simple sentences or fragments, they have a negative effect on both writing, language, and thinking skills.

Taking Time Without Giving Much in Return

Print and television are two media that compete for children's time and attention. But video is more seductive. Children frequently report finding television more life-like, easier and more desirable to spend time with than books. When similar groups have a chance to view or read about a particular subject they find the work harder with a book. Not only do they comprehend more about the subject when reading, but they are forced to conceptualize at a higher level or abstraction.

The behavior of parents is a key element in the media choices that children make. This behavior strongly influences whether or not a child reads, and how much or what they watch on television. Parental TV watching lends credibility to the medium in general. And their programming choices assert a strong influence when it comes to specific programs.

Although we typically spend twelve years preparing American children to deal critically with reading, we totally neglect teaching any critical TV viewing skills. And all of our graduates watch television—only half read. Pulling the plug is simply not practical so we have to learn to make the best of it. We may not want to increase the number of televiewing homes, but we **can** direct viewing habits and reap some cognitive benefits from viewing. If we dismiss video as unworthy of our attention then we may harm the child's ability to deal with a visually intensive future.

When Does Television Have a Positive Social or Educational Effect?

There are a few bright spots. For example, watching multicultural segments of Sesame Street increased preschoolers interest in playing with children from different ethnic backgrounds. Racial and ethnic differences on TV can be stereotyped by convenient stage mechanisms, but just as frequently television breaks down stereotypes.

To point out how ubiquitous American television has become and how it could contribute to global understanding we can look to **The Day After** (first broadcast in late 1983). The Russians who viewed the program (although it was not broadcast throughout the Soviet Union) reported being very moved by its content. This was one of the first programs where a large number of American parents and children watched a preselected program together—with educational advice from the National Education Association (NEA). Of course, intelligent TV viewing should not be limited to the few times that issues as powerful as nuclear war are dealt with. But this program did provide concrete evidence of what **can** happen when educators and parents work together on intellectually expanding television. By making the unthinkable thinkable, and abstract concepts concrete, **The Day After** is an example of the type of programming that can make a social and educational difference on a global level. Such programming might even serve as a small part of a process that could make a real impact on the future of humanity.

Interactive Television

Television (broadcast and cable) can perform a vital social-educational function in a world where ideas and information of the pictorial, print, and machine language variety zips between schools, homes, libraries, companies, and governmental agencies.

There are two new approaches that are now being successfully used to make television a more active tool for language learning. The first uses videodiscs and videodisc players connected to microcomputers. Children use this video technology to enter the Louvre in Paris or take a moon walk with the astronauts. They can stop the action, explore an object of interest slowly from any angle, and even call up print information that describes the conditions under which the artist created the painting, or the moon rock was retrieved. The production and viewing of art and science in this way can help demystify the concept of creativity and bring us closer to our environment.

The second approach to combining television, language activities and computing involves programs broadcast over the air. These programs, like PBS's **Voyage of the Mimi**, include booklets combining reading-writing activities and microcomputer diskettes that are sent to the schools.

Broadcast television offers some intelligent programming that can be viewed by older children and adults. But the seven to twelve year olds fall between the Sesame Street/Electric Company and the adult programming cracks (Nickelodeon and Disney are now on cable). It seems odd that even public broadcasting has no drama for children in this age group. The nature of American television is however influencing this age group throughout the world. The French news magaine, **Le Point**, has already carried a front page story for adolescent TV viewers (and others) entitled "Culture: How to Resist America."

American broadcasters need more of a chance to show imagination and intellectual depth for the entire spectrum of viewers around the world. Television writers, producers and programmers should be aware of their world-wide impact and be encouraged to do things they feel good about. Hopefully many of them will come to realize that we are all involved in selecting our future through the education of children.

When actual experience is not possible television may be the best means for influencing the imagination, intellect, and the aesthetic values of some children. Video is a powerful way to present information. And when it is coupled with informed interaction, either human or non human, it enables children to learn and grow.

As far as the educative potential of new media combinations are concerned, the jury has not even heard the evidence yet. Print, video, and computers may very well become complementary tools for learning. Computers run on electrical energy and the human brain on chemical energy. The human mind is not like a computer, but both transmit radio frequencies when they are functioning. And computers have the potential for controlling a type of hook up between the brain's computer and other media. Does this mean that computers will learn to read our thoughts? That will take some time—at the moment the best computer can't even read my handwriting. Like any experiment, the educational results of computer controlled video-human combinations will be viewed down the road, rather than at the beginning of the effort. Of one thing we can be certain, rapid new communication tools will have more direct access to our thinking process—and they are beginning to be tested. Some of these tools will have a major impact on personal, national, and the international nervous systems. Various forms of computer-based video will increasingly command world-wide attention. Once we clearly understand the most effective way to learn a subject we can teach a computer to do the teaching. Advances in artificial intelligence are resulting in microcomputer packages with decision making abilities comparable to any desired human model.

The computer-communications industries can set and accomplish the goals of contributing to the intellectual, aesthetic, and emotional maturity of viewers. To do this requires bringing together educators, media specialists and scholars from many interrelated fields to produce intelligent programs that appeal to children. This is particularly important now that computer controlled technology is starting to give us the opportunity for interacting with television in various ways—taking even more time away from print media and actual experience.

In different combinations with computer-based technology, TV can take on new dimensions that will give video even more attention getting power—and the potential for actively involving and expanding, rather than diminishing, human intellectual capacity. Although they have yet to be tapped, the technological opportunities for nurturing intelligent viewing are increasing at a surprising rate. This is especially true now that multinational companies (like IBM and AT&T) are in the process of designing new electronic networks where everything is linked to everything on a global basis. The whole thought producing process is poised for a quantum leap. It is time to consider how technology can be employed to eliminate illiteracy and ignorance—promoting human development on a world-wide basis.

"Programming" is the Weak Link in Creating a Global Exchange of Ideas

If you think that we are in the midst of profound technological experiment and change now, just wait a few years. A revolution in global communications and information distribution is about to get underway. IBM's recent alliance with CBS Broadcasting (for a nation-wide videotex service) and MCI Communications (the nation's second largest telephone service) and AT&T's move into computers (their Bell Labs were, after all, in on the invention of the transistor) recognize the need to merge the computer and communications industry. The result will be a global exchange of information and ideas that is beyond anything we can imagine today. Although transmitters in the brain are more chemical than electric their action can be connected to computers and adjusted in a number of ways. This whole process may be the greatest challenge humans have ever faced.

Language and patterns of thought, rather than computer skills, will be the key for dealing with the powerful synergism that results from the technological synthesis of software, computers, and communications. These new pipelines will carry moving images as well as data, print and voice. The mix involves fiber optics, cable, satellites, infared transmission, new switchboards (to direct traffic), new software (to make messages understood) and, most importantly, new programming.

With international competition a major force behind technological development it is important to come to terms with how people are manipulated. What exactly is the price, in human values, that we have to pay for our advances in science and technology? We have yet to come to grips with the potential social-educational implications of tapping these technological potentials. No one has spent much time looking at the effect of TV language and thinking on a mass audience—or the educative possibilities. It doesn't do us much good to have 155 channels of the same bland nonsense, no matter how much you can interact with it. And it certainly doesn't do other countries much good to suffer from this kind of cultural imperialism.

Part of the problem that television presents for influencing children's language skills is caused by the fact that the TV programmers see dialogue as simply a space filler between obligatory action scenes or canned laughter. They fail to recognize that one of the reasons that British television is more impressive than American TV is that their writers are taken seriously. Since the typical American video product has to follow a strict formula, hack writers do better than those who have some pride in their work. More than film, video lends itself to a narrative form.

There is a gap between how people throughout this world view education (idealistically) and the way differentiated opportunities that are the reality exist for most of them. Television, at the moment, is the common denominator. Our negligence in using it effectively is not trivial—in fact it points to how we may misuse future technologies. American communications programming doesn't feel responsible to its world-wide mass audience, many of whom can't or won't read. There has to be a little inclination to use writers, directors and producers who have both imagination and intellectual depth or otherwise it will continue to diminish human culture and language skills.

Figure 20. Computer Composite Image.

A Large Dose of Very Human Intelligence Must Guide the Technology

Television is a perfect example of how technology, by itself, cannot cultivate or improve human learning, nor human nature. And it certainly doesn't carry with it a moral or ethical code that automatically points towards an improvement in the human condition. Divorcing the search for technological possibilities from human values and intellectual concerns results in devices that steal our time, and the time of our children, without giving much in return. Our short sightedness allows an almost miraculous computer controlled technology—and the public airwaves—to be used (without much social conscience) for private profit. Far too often consideration of educative potential and public service is viewed (by insiders) as PR image building for the public and the FCC.

From the beginning, this country has recognized both the interconnection of technology, science, art, literature, education—and public funding. (All are now in the process of having their federal support cut.) President George Washington told Congress that: "There is nothing which better deserves your patronage than the promotion of science and literature." President John Quincy Adams also called for laws promoting "the cultivation and encouragement of the mechanic and the elegant arts, the advancement of literature, and the progress of the sciences." President John F. Kennedy quoted presidents Lincoln and Roosevelt when he said that technology, education, humanities, and the fine arts were "far from being a distraction in the life of a nation. They are close to the center of a nation's purpose—and a test of the quality of a nation's civilization."

Television is a primary means of involving most of our nation in the humanities today. Bad writing, sloppy language, and limited vision may be rampant in American video communications, but nothing, it seems, can diminish the time we spend with broadcast TV. And there is no way to predict the global influence of such work. But in its present form it is not likely to compel much human language or aesthetic development—or much thought.

As this medium merges with other technologies there is cause for concern. The problems that arise on the cutting edge of media technology involve not just the new communication-computer corporation alliances—but education, the arts, ethics, politics, psychology, medicine, biology and philosophy. Like all machines (some of which date back nearly 10,000 years) the computer is a mechanical device for capturing the power in nature. The potential is there for enabling the future. At issue here is nothing less than preventing a technologically induced dark age of perception and literacy. But there is not need to limit ourselves to prevention. Whether or not computers ever achieve a level of true consciousness they **can** become partners in teaching and learning. If we learn to manage today's technological miracles we could go on to set the stage for extending the potential of the human mind (on a global scale) in ways never before thought possible.

RESOURCES

Educational Computer Journals

AEDS MONITOR, Association for Educational Data Systems, 1201 Sixteenth Street, N.W., Washington, DC 20036.

Classroom Computer News, Intentional Educators, Inc., 51 Spring Street, Watertown, MA 02172, (617)923-7707.

COMPUTERS, READING and LANGUAGE ARTS, P.O. Box 13247, Oakland, CA 94661, (415)339-1106.

The Computing Teacher, Department of Computer and Information Sciences, University of Oregon, Eugene, OR 97403, (503)689-4414.

Educational Computer Magazine, P.O. Box 535, Cupertino, CA 95015, (408)252-3224.

Educational Computing, MAGSUB (Subscription Services) Ltd., Oakfield House, Perrymount Road, Haywards Heath, Sussex RH16 3DH, England.

Educational Technology, 140 Sylvan Avenue, Englewood Cliffs, NJ 07632, (201)871-4007.

Electronic Education, Communications, Inc., Suite 220, 1311 Executive Center Drive, Tallahassee, FL 32301, (904)878-4178.

Electronic Learning, Scholastic Inc., 902 Sylvan Avenue, Box 2001, Englewood Cliffs, NJ 07632, (201)567-7900.

Journal of Computer-Based Instruction, ADCIS, Computer Center, Western Washington University, Bellingham, WA 98225.

Journal of Educational Technology Systems, Baywood Publishing Company, Inc., 120 Marine St., Box D, Farmington, NY 11735, (516)249-7130.

MICROCOMPUTERS IN EDUCATION, Chapel Hill Drive, Fairfield, CT 06432.

MICRO-SCOPE, JEM Research, Discovery Park, University of Victoria, Box 1700, Victoria B.C. V8W 2Y2, Canada.

T.H.E. Journal, P.O. Box 992, Acton, MA 01720, (617)263-3607.

General Computing Periodicals

Byte, 70 Main Street, Peterborough, NH 03458, (603)924-9281.

Creative Computing, P.O. Box 789-M, Morristown, NJ 07960, (800)631-8112 and (210)540-0445.

Kilobaud Microcomputing, Subscription Department, P.O. Box 997, Farmingdale, NY 11737.

Personal Computer World c/o Steve England, 41 Rathbone Place, London W1P 1DE, England, (01)637-7991.
Personal Computing, P.O. Box 1408, Riverton, NJ 08077.
Popular Computing, 70 Main Street, Peterborough, NH 03458, (603)924-9281.

Sources of Critical Reviews of Educational Software

AMERICAN MICRO MEDIA, Box 306, Red Hood, NY 12571, (914)756-2557.
BOOKLIST, 50 East Huron Street, Chicago, IL 60611.
THE BOOK REPORT, Box 14466, Columbus, OH 43214.
COURSEWARE REPORT CARD, 150 West Carob Street, Compton, CA 90220.
DIGEST OF SOFTWARE REVIEWS: EDUCATION, 1341 Bulldog Lane, Suite C, Fresno, CA 93710.
EPIE MICRO-COURSEWARE, PRO/FILES, EPIE & Consumers Union, Box 620, Stony Brook, NY 11790.
JEM REFERENCE MANUAL, JEM Research, Discovery Park, University of Victoria, Box 1700, Victoria BC V8W 2Y2, Canada.
JOURNAL OF APPLE COURSEWARE REVIEW, Apple Computer Inc., Box 28426, San Jose, C A 95159.
MICRO MEDIA REVIEW, Box 125, Ridgefield, CT 06877.
MICROSIFT REVIEWS, Northwest Regional Educational Laboratory, 300 S.W. Sixth Avenue, Portland, OR 97204.

Educational Journals That Carry Occasional Articles on Computing

ARITHMETIC TEACHER, CURRICULUM REVIEW, 517 S. Jefferson St., Chicago, IL 60607.
EDUCATIONAL TECHNOLOGY, 140 Sylvan Ave., Englewood Cliffs, NJ 07632.
EPIE REPORT, Epie Institute, Box 620, Stony Brook, NY 11790.
INSTRUCTOR, 7 Bank Street, Dansville, NY 14437.
JOURNAL OF LEARNING DISABILITIES, 5615 West Cermak Road, Cicero, IL 60650.
LEARNING MAGAZINE, 530 University Ave., Palo Alto, CA 94301.
MATHEMATICS TEACHER, National Council of Teachers of Mathematics, 1906 Association Drive, Reston, VA 22091.
MEDIA & METHODS, 1511 Walnut Street, Philadelphia, PA 19102.

Newsletters from Computer Users' Groups

ATARI COMPUTER ENTHUSIASTS (Atari), 3662 Vine Maple Drive, Eugene, OR 97405.
CHICATRUG NEWS (TRS-80), Chicago TRS-80 Users Group, 203 N. Wabash, Room 1510, Chicago, IL 60601.

CUE NEWSLETTER, Computer-Using Educators, Box 18547, San Jose, CA 95158.

MACUL JOURNAL, Michigan Association for Computer Users in Learning, 33500 Van Born Rd., Wayne, MI 48184.

MIDNIGHT SOFTWARE GAZETTE (PET), Central Illinois PET Users' Group, 635 Maple Court, Mt. Zion, IL 62549.

USERS: THE MECC INSTRUCTIONAL COMPUTING NEWSLETTER, 2520 N. Broadway Drive, St. Paul, MN 55113.

Computer Journals That Carry Occasional Articles on Education

BYTE, 70 Main Street, Peterborough, NH 03458, (603)924-9281.

COMPUTE! Box 5406, Greensboro, NC 27403.

CREATIVE COMPUTING, Box 780-M, Morristown, NJ 07690.

80 MICROCOMPUTING (TRS-80), 80 Pine Street, Peterborough, NH 03458.

80 SOFTWARE CRITIQUE (TRS-80), Box 134, Waukegan, IL 60085.

INFOWORLD, 375 Cochituate Road, Box 800, Framington, MA 01701.

INTERFACE AGE, 16704 Marquardt Avenue, Cerritos, CA 90701.

INTERNATIONAL APPLE CORE, 908 George Street, Santa Clara, CA 95050.

MICROCOMPUTING, 80 Pine Street, Peterborough, NH 03458.

NIBBLE (Apple), Box 325, Lincoln, MA 01773.

PEELINGS II (Apple), 945 Brook Circle, Las Cruces, NM 88001.

PERSONAL COMPUTER AGE (IBM), 10057 Commercial Avenue, Tujunga, CA 91042.

PERSONAL COMPUTING, 50 Essex Street, Rochelle Park, NJ 07662.

POPULAR COMPUTING, 70 Main Street, Peterborough, NH 03458.

SOFTSIDE, Box 68, Milford, NH 03055.

SOFTALK MAGAZINE (Apple), 11021 Magnolia Boulevard, North Hollywood, CA 91601.

Some Books in Educational Computing

Ahuja, Vijay, *Design and Analysis of Computer Communication Networks*, McGraw-Hill, 1982.

Antebi, Elizabeth, *The Electronic Epoch*, Van Nostrand-Reinhold, 1983.

Bitter, Gary G., *Computers in Today's World*, Wiley, 1984.

Book of IBM Software, Addison-Welsey, 1984.

Brand, Steward (Ed.), *Whole Earth Software Catalog*, Quantum/Doubleday, 1984.

Christie, L., & Christie, J., *The Encyclopedia of Microcomputer Terminology*, Prentice-Hall, 1984.

Daiute, Colette, *Writing and Computers*, Addison-Wesley, 1984.

Feigenboum, Edward A., & McCorduck, Pamela, *The Fifth Generation*, Addison-Wesley, 1984.

Frank, Mary (Ed.), *Young Children in a Computerized Environment,* Haworth Press, 1982.
Fox, Joseph, M., *Software and Its Development*, Prentice-Hall, 1982.
Futrell, M., & Geisert, P., *The Well-Trained Computer*, Educational Technology Publications, 1984.
Geoffrin, Leo D., & Geoffrin, Olga P., *Computers and Reading Instruction,* Addison-Wesley, 1983.
Goldenberg, Paul E.; Russel, Susan Jo; & Carter, Cynthia J., *Computers, Education and Special Needs,* Addison-Wesley, 1984.
Glassner, Andrew S., *Computer Graphics User's Guide*, Bobbs-Merrill, 1984.
Guide to Personal Computing, Digital Press, 1982.
Hanson, Owen, *Design of Computer Data Files*, Computer Science Press, 1982.
Klingman, Edwin E., *Microprocessor Systems Design*, Vol. II, Prentice-Hall, 1982.
Lathrop, Ann & Goodson, Bobby, *Courseware in the Classroom*, Addison-Wesley, 1983.
Leggett, Stanton (Ed.), *Microcomputers Go to School*, Teach' Em, Inc., 1984.
Libes, Sol, *Fundamentals and Application of Digital Logic Circuits*, Hayden Book Company, 1980.
Marroquin, Raul, *The Link: Juan Maranas Political Campaign*, Maastricht Holland, 1982.
Mateosian, Richard, *Inside BASIC Games*, Sybex, 1981.
Math, Irwin, *Bits and Pieces*, Scribner, 1984.
Micro Data Base Systems, Inc., *Discovering KnowledgeMan*, Howard W. Sams, 1984.
Mitchell, Joyce Slayton, *Your Job in the Computer Age*, Scribner, 1984.
Papert, Seymour, *Mindstorms: Children, Computers and Powerful Ideas*, Basic Books, 1980.
Pasadena Technology Press, *Lee's Guide to Published Computer Programs,* 1984.
Prattis, Richard E., *Karel the Robot*, Wiley, 1981.
Peterson, Dale, *Big Things from Little Computers: A Layperson's Guide to Personal Computing*, Prentice-Hall, 1982.
Pitts, Gerald N., & Bateman, Barry L., *Essentials of COBOL Programming: A Structured Approach*, Computer Science Press, 1982.
Rappaport, Irwin, *Textedit*, Wayne Green, 1982.
Safford, Edward L., Jr., *The Complete Handbook of Robotics*, TAB Books, 1980.
Sigel, E., & Giglio, L., *Guide to Software Publishing*, Knowledge Industry Publications, 1984.
Simon, Herbert, *The Sciences of the Artificial* (2nd Ed.), MIT Press, 1981.
Sommer, Elyse, *Perfect Writer Made Perfectly Clear,* Chilton, 1984.
Spangenburg, R., & Moser, D., Personal Word Processing, Wadsworth, 1984.
Speitel, Tom, et al., *Science Computer Programs for Kids and Other People*, Reston, 1984.
Spencer, Donald, *Exploring the World of Computers*, Camelot, 1982.
Spencer, Donald, *Computer Dictionary for Everyone,* Scribner, 1984.
Turkle, Shelly, The Second Self: *Computers and the Human Spirit*, Simon & Schuster, 1984.
Willen, David C., *BASIC Programming with the IBM PCjr,* Howard Sams, 1984.
Willis, Jerry, & Johnson, D. LaMont, *Computers Teaching and Learning*, Dilithium Press, 1983.